The Fruit of the Spirit in You

Vince Rozier

ISBN-13: 9781707408139
STEP ONE Publishing

Unless otherwise noted, all Scripture quotations are taken from The Holy Bible, New King James Version, NKJV, copyright © 1982 by Thomas Nelson, Inc.

Otherwise quotations are from: New American Standard Bible **(NASB)** Copyright © 1995 by The Lockman Foundation; Contemporary English Version **(CEV)** Copyright © 1995 by American Bible Society; New Century Version **(NCV)** The Holy Bible, New Century Version®. Copyright © 2005 by Thomas Nelson, Inc.; King James Version **(KJV)**

In Bible verses at times the author italicizes words for emphasis.

Table of Contents

Introduction

Living a life that is pleasing to God should be the desire of every Christian. However, we are often distracted by the routines of our lives and fail to build a deeper relationship with God. We may even feel a challenge to prove our spirituality and knowledge about Christ. Meanwhile, we struggle to exemplify the life of someone who seeks to be more like Christ.

Instead of simply reciting bible verses and following the routines of our religion in order to prove our faith, it is time to show the fruit of God's Word in our lives. Instead of just talking about the Holy Spirit, it is time to live by the Spirit. What better place to start than with Galatians 5:22-23 and the fruit of the Spirit? In this passage, we have a description of a life that is guided by the Holy Spirit.

Such a life will display the fruit of love, joy, peace, patience, kindness, goodness, faithfulness, gentleness, and self-control. These seeds have been planted in every believer! However, producing this fruit takes work.

Over the course of the next 101 days, work to live a Spirit guided life. Take time and develop a closer relationship with God. *Reveal the Fruit of the Spirit in You!*

16 So I say, walk by the Spirit, and you will not gratify the desires of the flesh. 17 For the flesh desires what is contrary to the Spirit, and the Spirit what is contrary to the flesh. They are in conflict with each other, so that you are not to do whatever you want. 18 But if you are led by the Spirit, you are not under the law.

19 The acts of the flesh are obvious: sexual immorality, impurity and debauchery; 20 idolatry and witchcraft; hatred, discord, jealousy, fits of rage, selfish ambition, dissensions, factions 21 and envy; drunkenness, orgies, and the like. I warn you, as I did before, that those who live like this will not inherit the kingdom of God.

Galatians 5: 16-21

Fruit of the Spirit

> [22] *But the fruit of the Spirit is love, joy, peace, patience, kindness, goodness, faithfulness, [23] gentleness, self-control; against such things there is no law.*
>
> *NASB*

Galatians 5:22-23

As we work to become a woman or man after God's own heart, one powerful passage in particular stands out. It provides us with insight to becoming the finished product. In Galatians 5:22-23, not only do we discover what traits we will possess when we are guided by the Spirit, but we also learn that the seeds that produce these traits have already been planted in us.

The Holy Spirit has implanted in us the seeds of *love, joy, peace, patience, kindness, goodness, faithfulness, gentleness, and self-control*. Each day, we have the opportunity to reveal to the world that not only do we possess these seeds, but that we are actually producing fruit.

So, let us ask ourselves, are we truly working to produce Godly fruit, or are we working to produce fruit that honors our own desires and personal endeavors? Are we working to reveal the fruit of the seeds instilled in each of us who receives the Holy Spirit, or are we producing fruit that only glorifies ourselves?

2

Over the next one hundred days, let us become more focused on revealing the fruit of the Holy Spirit in our day to day actions. Let us work to live a life that reflects our commitment to God. Let us pray to be filled with and guided by the Holy Spirit.

Day 1

_____

_____

_____

_____

_____

_____

_____

_____

_____

_____

_____

_____

_____

Love

Joy

Peace

Patience

Kindness

Goodness

Faithfulness

Gentleness

Self-control

CHAPTER 1

Fruit

16 You will know them by their fruits. Do men gather grapes from thornbushes or figs from thistles? 17 Even so, every good tree bears good fruit, but a bad tree bears bad fruit. 18 A good tree cannot bear bad fruit, nor can a bad tree bear good fruit. 19 Every tree that does not bear good fruit is cut down and thrown into the fire. 20 Therefore by their fruits you will know them.

Matthew 7: 16-20

Fruit   Day 2

> **By this My Father is glorified, that you bear much fruit; so you will be My disciples.**

John 15:8

Many parents have reminded their children to be good representatives of the family when away from home. They teach their children that poor behavior by one member of the family reflects negatively on the entire family. If this principle is true, what message do we present for those who know that we follow and believe in an almighty God?

Are the fruit of the Spirit evidenced in us in ways that honor God? Do our interactions show the *joy* we have because we follow the ways of a heavenly Father that *loves* us all? Do we display *peace* and *patience* during our ups and downs because we are *faithful* and know that God has dominion over all? Do our actions model the **kindness, goodness,** and **gentleness** of Christ? Do we follow our Savior who was crucified so that we all may have eternal life, regardless of our past sins during times when we lost our *self-control*?

Unless we remain connected to God, we will struggle to honor Him. When we are disconnected from Him, we cannot produce His fruit. Let us remain plugged-in and broadcast to all that He deserves the honor, glory, and praise. Let us reveal the fruit of the Spirit in us.

Day 2

_____

_____

_____

_____

_____

_____

_____

_____

_____

_____

_____

_____

_____

_____

_____

_____

_____

_____

_____

_____

Fruit   Day 3

> *So God created man in His own image; in the image of*
> *God He created him; male and female He created them.*

Genesis 1:27

Throughout our lives, we often search to uncover what path God would have us to follow. The success of Pastor Rick Warren's book *The Purpose Driven Life* serves as an example of how much we desire to know what God has purposed and intended for our lives.[1] As with any journey, though, it is important to recognize where we first began in order to understand how to arrive at our final destination.

We began as creations of God, made in His own image. However, in our journeys, we often reveal traits of apples that have fallen far from the tree (of life). Because we were created in the image of God, our lives should reflect the character of God. We should aim to have others observe our actions and know that we are children of God.

Instead of giving our attention to the physical image of God, let us focus on the character of who He is. The image of God is not simply his physical appearance, rather it is what we know of His power, grace, mercy, eternal salvation, etc. Let us work to have others see this image of God in the fruit of our spirit.

---

[1] Warren, Rick (2002). *The Purpose Driven Life*. Michigan: Zondervan.

Day 3

_____

_____

_____

_____

_____

_____

_____

_____

_____

_____

_____

_____

_____

_____

_____

_____

_____

_____

_____

Fruit   Day 4

> **Therefore, if anyone is in Christ, he is a new creation; old things have passed away; behold, all things have become new.**

2 Corinthians 5:17

There are television shows dedicated to performing a make-over on people, houses, and businesses. Children often ask for a do-over when playing games. Adults often wish for the opportunity to make-up for past mistakes or undo past acts. While we cannot change things from our past, we are able to change the path of our eternal future.

If we allow, Christ will remove the burdens that have weighed us down, guide us forward from our errant behaviors, and reveal the path away from our addictions. He will ignore the failures from our past that may still embarrass us in the present. He will see us as new beings and forgive our sins. Through our belief, we allow Christ to present us as the person He intended for us to be. In this newness, the fruit of our actions may now be more like Him.

Let us learn to forgive ourselves, as Christ has forgiven us. Let us acknowledge Him and see ourselves as new creations in Him. Let us produce fresh fruit. Through His grace, we can allow all old things to pass away and live a fresh, new life in Him.

Day 4

_____

_____

_____

_____

_____

_____

_____

_____

_____

_____

_____

_____

_____

_____

_____

_____

_____

_____

<u>Fruit</u>   Day 5

I press toward the goal for the prize of the upward call of God in Christ Jesus.

Philippians 3:14

Runners who have completed a marathon do not spontaneously get up and run 26.2 miles. They begin with shorter distances and work their way up to race day. Likewise, babies do not learn to walk without countless attempts and falls. Even learning to ride a bicycle requires its share of bumps and bruises. It is often the same in our Christian walk.

Romans 3:23 tells us that we "all have sinned and fall short of the glory of God." That is no reason, however, for us to give up in our endeavor to press toward heaven's call. The fruit we produce may not always be that of the Holy Spirit. At times, the fruit we produce may even appear rotten. However, because of the sacrifice of Christ, we may be forgiven. Because of Christ, we can still be renewed and produce spiritual fruit that is fresh and ripe.

So, let us not become discouraged or deterred by our temporary failings, but encouraged by the promise of eternity. Let us continue to press forward toward the prize of our higher calling.

Day 5

_____

_____

_____

_____

_____

_____

_____

_____

_____

_____

_____

_____

_____

_____

_____

_____

_____

_____

Fruit   Day 6

> **_As in water face reflects face, So a man's heart reveals the man._**

Proverbs 27:19

It has been said that it is not wise to shop for groceries on an empty stomach because the eyes and stomach do more of the shopping than the head. Without discipline, but with the available money, everything the eyes and stomach desire may end up in the shopping cart. Like our eyes and stomachs, our hearts can reveal the things we crave and desire.

So, instead of only associating nutrition with our physical diet, we also should focus on feeding our hearts with balanced spiritual meals that make us strong. Just as we may step onto a scale and decide to change the way we eat, we can also pray about what excesses we should drop from our hearts. Matters such as our lust, anger, or envy may not be seen with the naked eye. However, such things make us spiritually unhealthy and slow down our spiritual growth.

Let us subscribe to a daily spiritual fitness plan in our efforts to be more pleasing to God. We can become spiritually stronger when we exercise our faith by reading, praying, and meditating on the Lord and His Word each day. So, let us work to have hearts that reveal our spiritual strength and connection Christ.

Day 6

_____

_____

_____

_____

_____

_____

_____

_____

_____

_____

_____

_____

_____

_____

_____

_____

_____

_____

Fruit   Day 7

Show me Your ways, O LORD; Teach me Your paths.

Psalm 25:4

The influence of peers on a young person is often strong. For instance, when a teenager begins to associate with a positive or negative group of peers, he or she often begins to dress and use similar language as those in the group. This effect is not exclusive to teens.

Many adults seek acceptance by becoming members of and attending particular churches, restaurants, social clubs, and charitable organizations, because they want to be associated with certain people. Current trends or styles may influence what we choose to wear. We may even allow political affiliations and public opinion to guide our thoughts, even if contrary to the ways of Christ. Instead of being like others, let us ask for God to show us His ways and teach them to us.

Who and what is popular will change. Styles and cultures will fluctuate. However, God's Word is eternal and solid. What we desire nor what our friends believe will always be the same as God's ways. However, let us ask for God to reveal to us His eternal ways. Let us learn His ways so that we will not be led astray.

Day 7

_____

_____

_____

_____

_____

_____

_____

_____

_____

_____

_____

_____

_____

_____

_____

_____

_____

_____

Fruit   Day 8

> [15] *Beware of false prophets, who come to you in sheep's clothing, but inwardly they are ravenous wolves.* [16] *You will know them by their fruits . . .*

Matthew 7:15-16

Emergency vehicles have sirens. Large trucks often beep when backing up. Warnings scroll across the bottom of our televisions to warn of threatening weather. However, there is no common device to place us on guard when false prophets approach us proclaiming things in the name of God.

With a silver tongue, they use the name of God to speak to our disappointments, insecurities, or loneliness. They may even try to tempt us away from what we know to be the true Word of God. In these encounters, we may find ourselves confused as to the proper direction for our lives. So, we pray for clarity, seeking an answer. All the while, we wonder if this is divine assistance from God or a false prophet.

Though we may not have mechanically-designed spiritual warning systems, we do have the Spirit to guide us. Let us cling to the Word of God and develop a regular relationship with God. Let us abide in the Sprit, so that we may be able to hear and recognize the guidance of that still, small voice directing our paths.[2] Let us stay focused on our eternal God and not on the appeal of temporary glamour. Let us exemplify that we are true followers of Christ.

---

[2] 1 Kings 19:12, King James Version (KJV)

Day 8

_____

_____

_____

_____

_____

_____

_____

_____

_____

_____

_____

_____

_____

_____

_____

_____

_____

_____

_____

Fruit   Day 9

> **⁸ *For if these things are yours and abound, you will be neither barren nor unfruitful in the knowledge of our Lord Jesus Christ. ⁹ For he who lacks these things is shortsighted, even to blindness, and has forgotten that he was cleansed from his old sins.***

2 Peter 1:8-9

Because Christ gave His life, we have access to the forgiveness of our sins! However, knowing this fact does not prevent us from remembering our past faults, even though they have been forgiven. We may struggle to move forward because we feel chained to the weights of our past. With these weights, we are restrained from being fully fruitful. This is not the behavior of someone who is free in Christ, but of someone who is still a slave, shackled by sin.

Let us remember that through Christ, we may be freed from the weight of our failures, embarrassments, and former choices. When we are focused on all that Christ has done for us, we have the tools to be fruitful. Christ allows our pains to be removed through his spiritual surgery, yet we remain whole. That place of pain may be replaced and filled with the Holy Spirit's comfort.

Like the music artist Lecrae, let us proclaim, "I volunteer for your sanctifying surgery. I know the Spirit's purging me of everything that's hurting me."[3] Let us be purged so that we may grow in Christ.

---

[3] Lecrae, *Boasting* (Rehab, 2010).

Day 9

_____

_____

_____

_____

_____

_____

_____

_____

_____

_____

_____

_____

_____

_____

_____

_____

_____

_____

_____

Fruit   Day 10

Therefore bear fruits worthy of repentance,   **NKJV**

Do the things that show you really have changed your hearts and lives.   **New Century Version**

Matthew 3:8

In most places, it is possible to recognize the season of the year by simply stepping outside, feeling the temperature, looking at the foliage, and observing the weather. In the third chapter of Matthew, John proclaimed to the Pharisees and Sadducees who came to him, that they should not settle for the outward sign of change present in baptism. Instead, like the changing of seasons from winter to spring, there should be an observable change in their hearts and lives. We, too, should have our commitment to Christ reflected in our interactions with others.

John challenges us not to be hypocritical in our faith. However, we will never prove that we are worthy of the repentance that God has graciously provided, no matter how hard we try. Yet, let us endeavor to follow Christ's teachings and manifest the fruit of someone who is saved. John described this as bearing fruits worthy of repentance.

With each day, let us draw closer to God and project to the world that He is in our hearts. It does not matter where or when we accepted Christ. It does not matter what we have done. We all will continue to fall short. So, let us simply strive to separate ourselves from things that are unlike Christ.

Day 10

_____

_____

_____

_____

_____

_____

_____

_____

_____

_____

_____

_____

_____

_____

_____

_____

_____

_____

_____

_____

Love

Joy

Peace

Patience

Kindness

Goodness

Faithfulness

Gentleness

Self-control

CHAPTER 2

Spirit

¹⁶ And I will pray the Father, and He will give you another Helper, that He may abide with you forever— ¹⁷ the Spirit of truth, whom the world cannot receive, because it neither sees Him nor knows Him; but you know Him, for He dwells with you and will be in you.

John 14:16-17

> *But the Helper, the Holy Spirit, whom the Father will send in My name, He will teach you all things, and bring to your remembrance all things that I said to you.*

John 14:26

Even after our days of school are over, we continue to face pop quizzes on a regular basis. But instead of exams on reading, writing, or math, we must deal with personal, spiritual, and emotional tests that can hold us back. To help us succeed on our spiritual journey, we have the Holy Spirit. He is described as a comforter, helper, advocate, and friend.

The Holy Spirit has been sent by God the Father to us and for us. When we are in need, the ever present voice of the Holy Trinity is there. Not only does He teach us, but He will help us remember all those words from Christ on which we may so desperately lean.

There may be times when we feel lonely. There may be times when we truly want a friend to help us endure the difficult times in our lives. Let us rejoice in knowing that we have our comforter and helper there with us, and we are not alone.

Day 11

_____

_____

_____

_____

_____

_____

_____

_____

_____

_____

_____

_____

_____

_____

_____

_____

_____

_____

_____

_____

Spirit   Day 12

> *The Spirit of the LORD is upon Me, Because He has anointed Me To preach the gospel to the poor; He has sent Me to heal the brokenhearted, To proclaim liberty to the captives And recovery of sight to the blind, To set at liberty those who are oppressed;*

Luke 4:18

"The devil made me do it," was a phrase made popular by the comedian Flip Wilson during his 1970s award winning variety television series.[4] In various skits, one character (Geraldine) would use this phrase to explain her misguided actions. Likewise, many of us seem to explain our actions by placing blame on the devil for choices that we have made. How would our lives be today if we were to live by the phrase, "The Spirit made me do it"?

Jesus explained that with the anointing of the Spirit, He preached, healed, and actively liberated those bound by sin. We, too, may pour blessings into the lives of others when we follow the instruction of the Holy Spirit. Whether by volunteering, encouraging others, or simply listening to someone's problems, there are countless ways we may respond to the anointing of the Spirit.

Has the Spirit directed you to act? If so, have you followed your instructions? What Spirit-guided fruit have

---

[4] *The Flip Wilson Show.* Prod. Robert Henry. NBC. Stage 1, NBC Studios, Burbank, California. 1970. Television.

been produced? To whom has the Spirit sent you to go and speak? Where has the Spirit guided you to go? It may be time to get going!

Day 12

_____

_____

_____

_____

_____

_____

_____

_____

_____

_____

_____

_____

_____

_____

> *¹ There is therefore now no condemnation to those who are in Christ Jesus, who do not walk according to the flesh, but according to the Spirit. ² For the law of the Spirit of life in Christ Jesus has made me free from the law of sin and death.*

Romans 8:1-2

Guilt, shame, disappointment, embarrassment . . . these are just a few of the emotions we may feel when we sin. Knowing that we have not met our personal standards or (most importantly) God's standard, can leave us feeling low because we recognize our failures. As Paul described in Romans 7:24, we feel like wretched or miserable beings. We do, however, have a rescue from this condemnation. Our salvation comes from the life we find through Christ.

Through Christ, we may be guided by the Spirit away from a focus on pleasing our egos, our bodies, or other people. In moments of indecision, the Spirit will guide us to victory. Conversely, even when we stray from our proper path, we still have access to victory through Christ because of the forgiveness of our sins and God's grace. We do not have to feel condemned, for we can be more than conquerors through Christ. Our victory serves as a fruit of a life in Christ.

We should not think, however, that because of victory in Christ that we are free to please ourselves. Instead, let us sincerely choose to follow the Spirit's lead away from our temptations and toward what is pleasing to God.

Day 13

_____

_____

_____

_____

_____

_____

_____

_____

_____

_____

_____

_____

_____

_____

_____

_____

_____

_____

<u>Spirit</u>   Day 14

> *For he who sows to his flesh will of the flesh reap*
> *corruption, but he who sows to the Spirit will of the*
> *Spirit reap everlasting life.*

Galatians 6:8

If asked about the priorities in our lives, we typically would answer God is first. Most people then may follow up with family, then work. While that is the answer we would state, what conclusion would be reached from an observation of our lives on a day to day basis?

Do we go through the motions of religious exercises but fail to work-out our spiritual muscles in order to grow stronger in our faith? Would it appear that we are more concerned with our reputation and outer appearance than we are with allowing the Spirit to be seen through us? Would an observer find that we easily give in to our frustrations, temptations, and other negative emotions?

Instead of choosing to satisfy our emotions or bodies, let us seek to sow seeds that allow us to have a greater fellowship with the Spirit. We may acquire temporary praise or satisfaction on earth when we reap of the flesh. However, let us look to reap the eternal rewards that come by way of the Spirit. Let us sow and receive eternal and spiritual blessings.

Day 14

_____

_____

_____

_____

_____

_____

_____

_____

_____

_____

_____

_____

_____

_____

_____

_____

_____

_____

_____

> *For those who live according to the flesh set their minds on the things of the flesh, but those who live according to the Spirit, the things of the Spirit.*

Romans 8:5

One phrase that has become popular in recent years speaks of "being in the zone." When someone is in the zone, their mind is completely focused on the task at hand. "Being in the zone" requires that one follow through on that mindset in both word and deed.

We have the option to choose whether to be in the zone of the flesh or the Spirit. Those who have their minds set on things of the flesh will pursue selfish pleasures and follow a life that is void of the Spirit. This life may impress many others. The self-gratifying lifestyle has its temptations, but it ultimately is unfulfilling. However, those who choose to live by the Spirit will enjoy fellowship with God and reveal the fruit of the Spirit in them.

Instead of seeking to satisfy our emotional and physical instincts and desires, let us strive to maintain a spiritual mindset. Let us stay in a spiritual zone, endeavoring to please God.

Day 15

_____

_____

_____

_____

_____

_____

_____

_____

_____

_____

_____

_____

_____

_____

_____

_____

_____

_____

> *23 But the hour is coming, and now is, when the true worshipers will worship the Father in spirit and truth; for the Father is seeking such to worship Him. 24 God is Spirit, and those who worship Him must worship in spirit and truth.*

John 4:23-24

Our Almighty God is not limited like a physical being. He is so great and grand that He cannot be encompassed by any material measurement. It is through the spiritual nature of God that He is fully omnipotent. Even more, it is through the spiritual nature that we have the Trinity of Father, Son, and Holy Spirit.

Because God is Spirit, we should worship Him spiritually. Jewish traditions involved physical ceremonies, rituals, and procedures that were utilized for worship. Jesus, however, taught that we are to worship in spirit and truth.

Worshipping God in truth does not come down to ceremonies but is a way of life. A life of worship involves sincerity and integrity, not hypocrisy. We can spend ample time trying to conform to traditional practices because that is the way it's always been done. Jesus did not protest finding methods that are comfortable for worship. However, simply going through the routines and motions are not enough.

Let us worship our Spirit God, with a spiritual worship. Let us allow our spiritual worship to be evident by living a life of worship.

Day 16

_____

_____

_____

_____

_____

_____

_____

_____

_____

_____

_____

_____

_____

_____

_____

_____

_____

<u>Spirit</u>   Day 17

> **Now the Lord is the Spirit; and where the Spirit of the Lord is, there is liberty.**

2 Corinthians 3:17

Throughout generations, the concept of bondage has been represented by the image of chains. Chains do not completely restrict a prisoner's movement. However, any time there is an attempt to move too far away from a point, the chains bind the prisoner to some structure or weight. Even without a physical attachment or chain, many of us are restricted by mindsets and emotional weights that prevent us from moving forward in our lives. There is hope, however, in the Spirit!

The Spirit will guide us to freedom and teach us how to overcome our circumstances. The Spirit will reveal to us that we have the power to overcome and break the chains that hold us back. No matter if these are chains of disappointment, abuse, addiction, or temptation, the Spirit will reveal to us the path to overcome.

Let us refuse to be held back by personal injuries from the past, whether physical or emotional. Let us choose to fight beyond issues of our present and not give in to disappointments from the past. Let us claim the freedom that is waiting for us.

Day 17

_____

_____

_____

_____

_____

_____

_____

_____

_____

_____

_____

_____

_____

_____

_____

_____

_____

> ***And take the helmet of salvation, and the sword of the Spirit, which is the word of God;***

Ephesians 6:17

In the past, warriors and soldiers were fully loaded with armor when going into battle, but there was only one traditional weapon used to go on the offensive, the sword. Usually short and made for intense, close, and quick response encounters, one had to be familiar with his sword or lose his fight. Even more, the sword was double edged. So, if the person using the sword was unskilled, he might cut himself. Finally, a warrior or soldier never intentionally released his sword until the battle was over.

It is easy to see why the (s)Word of God is given to us as our primary tool to defeat Satan's attempts to lead us astray. When we use scripture to resist Satan, just as Christ did in the fourth chapter of Matthew, we too can escape Satan's traps. One appropriately applied scripture is better than any philosophy or motivational quote. It also reveals to others that they, too, should learn from our sword fighting instructor.

We can make sure that we are well trained, by taking the time to learn and apply the Spirit inspired words of our bibles. When we put on the full armor of God, we can do more than just prepare to protect ourselves. We can become skilled, scripture-wielding believers, who are prepared to take on Satan. All we have to do is take the time and train.

Day 18

_____

_____

_____

_____

_____

_____

_____

_____

_____

_____

_____

_____

_____

_____

_____

_____

_____

_____

_____

_____

<u>Spirit</u>   Day 19

⁴ There is one body and one Spirit, just as you were called in one hope of your calling; ⁵ one Lord, one faith, one baptism;   ⁶ one God and Father of all, who is above all, and through all, and in you all.

Ephesians 4:4-6

What church do you attend? What denomination are you? What style of music is played at your church? What kind of people attend your church? There are numerous ways in which we choose to separate ourselves when worshipping the one true God.

Much of what we desire in a worship experience may relate to the traditions we became accustomed to in our early Christian years. Yet, because we are comfortable with our style of worship, there may be a temptation to denigrate the worship, works, and evangelism of others. We forget that though we do not use the same means, we all desire the same results. No matter our heritage, job, house size, music style or dress, we must remember that we all are a part of one body of Christ.

There is one Lord in whom we have faith, and we are free to serve our God through fellowship with all. As the body of Christ, it is time that we show our daily worship with heaven in mind, without concern for fitting in. Instead of focusing on our differences, let us focus on doing the Lord's work. Let us focus on our service to God as a form of worship.

Day 19

_____

_____

_____

_____

_____

_____

_____

_____

_____

_____

_____

_____

_____

_____

_____

_____

_____

_____

_____

Love

Joy

Peace

Patience

Kindness

Goodness

Faithfulness

Gentleness

Self-control

CHAPTER 3

Love

34 A new commandment I give to you, that you love one another; as I have loved you, that you also love one another. 35 By this all will know that you are My disciples, if you have love for one another."

John 13:34-35

Love   Day 20

> *You shall love the LORD your God with all your heart,*
> *with all your soul, and with all your strength.*

Deuteronomy 6:5   Matthew 22:36

True love is more than a mere emotion. It is a verb that is evidenced by our actions, words, and attitude. For example, caring for someone but not following through in action is merely affection, not love. Thus, while we love all that God has done for us, we should actively express our love for Him as a verb, and not just profess our appreciation.

In loving God, we may praise, respect, and follow Him. When we choose to live our lives and carry ourselves in ways contrary to the ways of God, we do not love Him. We reveal our love with our daily speech or even in our silence. However, just as in a marriage, we fail to properly love when we put something or someone else above the one to whom we should be committed.

Let us refuse to put anything ahead of our love for God. We cannot serve two masters. Our desire for praise and acclaim may stand in our way of loving God. A love for money or pleasure will also hinder our relationship with God. Instead, let us remain focused and be committed to our God and love Him.

Day 20

_____

_____

_____

_____

_____

_____

_____

_____

_____

_____

_____

_____

_____

_____

_____

_____

_____

_____

_____

_____

Love   Day 21

> *For God so loved the world that He gave His only begotten Son, that whoever believes in Him should not perish but have everlasting life.*

John 3:16

Humanity can be inhumane. In every century, there have been attempts to lessen the value of certain individuals. Today, certain people are still demeaned due to their race, income, nationality, gender, lifestyle, etc.

On occasion, those who are different are presented as having lives of lesser value than others. Even in news reports about distant wars or events nearby, the deaths of certain individuals are often reported as being less newsworthy than others. When it comes to sin, some Christians even seem to suggest that people who have committed specific acts, have various addictions, or have lived certain lifestyles are unworthy of salvation.

While we continue to attribute value based on particular categories, God subscribes to a different valuation strategy. God has a *whoever* valuation approach. No matter the origin, history, past mistakes, or present circumstances, *whoever* believes in Christ has everlasting life. God so loved the whole world that he made salvation available to *whoever*.

Do you live by a *whoever* kind of love and treat others with love, *whoever* they are? Do you love beyond biological, social, and economic barriers? Can you see beyond sin to love a sinner? Falling short of living by God's standard does not stop God from loving us. What is your excuse? Let us all learn to have a *whoever* kind of love.

Day 21

_____

_____

_____

_____

_____

_____

_____

_____

_____

_____

_____

_____

_____

_____

_____

Love
Day 22

> *Love never fails. But whether there are prophecies, they will fail; whether there are tongues, they will cease; whether there is knowledge, it will vanish away.*

1 Corinthians 13:8

The love of a parent towards a child is unique. Through ups and downs, successes and failures, and all types of circumstances, parents tend to continue loving their child, no matter the the child's indiscretions. This power of love can be seen in God's love towards us.

Paul writes that the spiritual gift of love never fails and persists through various circumstances. Prophecies, tongues, and knowledge may fail or no longer be necessary. God's love towards us, however, is everlasting.

So, why don't we take the time to have an ongoing love toward others? Through love, we have the opportunity to help others in need, to seek peace with enemies, and to rebuild relationships. Love can serve as an unfailing engine for us to do God's will.

Because the gift of love never fails, there is comfort in knowing that God's love for us will always prevail. Therefore, let us remember that no matter the circumstances and no matter our failings, there will always be an opportunity for us to show love to others. Because we know that love never fails, let us not fail to love.

Day 22

_____

_____

_____

_____

_____

_____

_____

_____

_____

_____

_____

_____

_____

_____

_____

_____

_____

_____

_____

Love   Day 23

> *Greater love has no one than this, than to lay down one's life for his friends.*

John 15:13

It is easy to become focused on the busyness of life. By the time we are finished doing the things we have to do, there often is little time left for the things we want to do. For some, work becomes the singular focus of life. It seems that they live to work. For others, their lives revolve around their time away from work. They proclaim that they live for the weekend, television, or whatever relaxes them.

Christ laid down more than all of this in His sacrifice for us. He gave His actual life. Instead of living for work or for the weekend, He lived and died for us.

What are you willing to put aside to show the love that you have for others? Our culture tells us that there is nothing wrong with keeping the focus on ourselves. Jesus, however, leads by example. He tells us that there is no better way to show our love than to lay down our lives for another.

It is unlikely that we will face the challenge of physically giving our life for another. The question does remain, though, what are you willing to put aside to help another? Are you willing to give up time at work or time in front of the television to help another? What are you willing to give up to lead someone else to Jesus?

Day 23

_____

_____

_____

_____

_____

_____

_____

_____

_____

_____

_____

_____

_____

_____

_____

_____

_____

_____

Love   Day 24

> ¹⁸ *My little children, let us not love in word or in tongue, but in deed and in truth.* ¹⁹ *And by this we know that we are of the truth, and shall assure our hearts before Him.*

1 John 3:18-19

Real life stories of abuse and domestic violence are becoming more exposed with each passing year. Commonly, the excuse of love is provided as a faulty explanation provided by parents who abuse their children and by spouses who perpetrate physical and verbal violence towards another spouse. These abusers fail to recognize that love is not simply spoken, but is shown.

Speaking the word love does not equate with the real quality of love that should exist in our actions and hearts. While we, hopefully, do not go to the extreme of abuse, we too can look to our actions to examine whether we truly show love to those around us. For many, the problem is not in showing appropriate love to associates in public. The problem is in showing and acting out love to those who are closest to us. Let us aim to reveal a Christ-like loving spirit to all.

Christ showed His love for us and took abuse for us. He did not abuse others. Because of what Christ did, we know the pure heart of the Son. What would an examination of our hearts reveal about our love? Do your actions show the fruit of love?

Day 24

_____

_____

_____

_____

_____

_____

_____

_____

_____

_____

_____

_____

_____

_____

_____

_____

_____

_____

Love

> **10 In this is love, not that we loved God, but that He loved us and sent His Son to be the propitiation for our sins. 11 Beloved, if God so loved us, we also ought to love one another.**

1 John 4:10-11

The beginning of a long term dating relationship often follows a common pattern. As two people get to know one another, the two share their thoughts and seek ways to express their affection. This may be with cards, gifts, or kind words to express a growing connection. However, instead of sending chocolate or flowers, God showed His love for us by sending His Son to suffer on our behalf.

There are many things we may think of asking for, but Christ gave us the unimaginable gift of His love. Now, we have the opportunity to live our lives loving Him after He first loved us. Just as with others, we can show God our love. We do this by living lives that are pleasing to Him.

It pleases God when we love others, regardless of who that person is. No matter what a person or group has done or what those around us say or believe, we have received spiritual instruction. We are to love.

There is no need to take an offering of sacrifice (or chocolates) to God now in order to receive forgiveness. If God loved us so much to send His Son, let us show our love for God and love one another.

Day 25

_____

_____

_____

_____

_____

_____

_____

_____

_____

_____

_____

_____

_____

_____

_____

_____

_____

_____

_____

<u>Love</u>   Day 26

Since you have purified your souls in obeying the truth
through the Spirit in sincere love of the brethren, love
one another fervently with a pure heart,

---

1 Peter 1:22

Years ago, who would have imagined that there would be so many different types of water: sparkling, distilled, spring, mineral, etc.? Each claims to hold its own purities and benefits. None, however, will change the way a person thinks or treats others, unlike the purity of the Holy Spirit.

In accepting Christ and receiving the Holy Spirit, our wrongs are forgiven. Our sins are erased. With this cleansing, the filth of our past is distilled and filtered from our hearts. God treats us as if we never committed any sin before in our lives; but how do we treat others?

Do we treat others with pre-conceived notions? Do we respond to others based on lessons we learned during sinful experiences in our past? Have we learned to treat people as a response to the mistreatment that we received from others? Have we succumbed to insecurities we have developed because of sin, or do we, instead, interact with others with a pure desire to love?

Let us choose to separate ourselves from sinfulness and its after-effects, just as Christ separated us from sin when He died on the cross. Let us remove the stained fingerprints of sin that affect our interactions with others. Let us love others with pure hearts.

Day 26

_____

_____

_____

_____

_____

_____

_____

_____

_____

_____

_____

_____

_____

_____

_____

_____

_____

_____

Love   Day 27

> *He who loves his life will lose it, and he who hates his life in this world will keep it for eternal life.*

John 12:25

What is truly important to you? Many of us are focused on achieving goals simply to keep up with others or to say what we have accomplished. Some are obsessed with attaining more money and possessions, so that they (and others) can look and see all they have done. Others want more free time to only do things that make them happy, no matter the impact. We may even feel pressured to change our opinions about following God's Word because we find it important not to be considered religious relics, living in modern times.

Ultimately, our principles and how we use our time, talents, and money, will reveal what is truly important in our lives. What will our receipts, schedules, and associations, say about what we deem to be significant? Just as in a criminal investigation, the evidence will leave a trail to the truth.

The evidence surrounding Christ shows that He left a trail of blood and sweat as He carried the cross on His way to be crucified. In love, He gave His life that we all may have eternal life and forgiveness. We must decide, for whom and for what we are living. When we take an account, we may discover that we are forsaking our eternal lives only to glorify our earthly lives. Let us not love our lives so much that we forsake our life creator.

In You

Day 27

_____

_____

_____

_____

_____

_____

_____

_____

_____

_____

_____

_____

_____

_____

_____

_____

_____

Love   Day 28

> [44] *But I say to you, love your enemies, bless those who curse you, do good to those who hate you, and pray for those who spitefully use you and persecute you* [45] *that you may be sons of your Father in heaven; for He makes His sun rise on the evil and on the good, and sends rain on the just and on the unjust.* [46] *For if you love those who love you, what reward have you? Do not even the tax collectors do the same?* [47] *And if you greet your brethren only, what do you do more than others? Do not even the tax collectors do so?* [48] *Therefore you shall be perfect, just as your Father in heaven is perfect.*

Matthew 5:44-48

Following the Spirit requires that we not follow human nature, but instead, follow a spiritual and Godly nature. According to worldly and human nature, it is fine to hate someone, especially if we consider that person an enemy. In fact, the world suggests that it is appropriate to hate your neighbor, co-worker, or any other person who says spiteful things about you or stands in your way.

When we live according to the Spirit, however, we do not live by human nature, but Jesus' nature. Jesus taught us that instead of hating, we should love. We should love others regardless of what has been said about us or done to us. Love will motivate us to turn around and pray for those who are against us.

Loving those whom we feel do not deserve our love is being like Christ. We could never be worthy of His salvation and grace, but He still loves us. Regardless of whether anyone else sees it or not, let us desire to love others as Christ loved us. Let us reveal the fruit of the Spirit in us through our love for others.

Day 28

_____

_____

_____

_____

_____

_____

_____

_____

_____

_____

_____

_____

_____

Love

Joy

Peace

Patience

Kindness

Goodness

Faithfulness

Gentleness

Self-control

CHAPTER 4

Joy

But let all those rejoice

who put their trust in You;

Let them ever shout for joy,

because You defend them;

Let those also who love Your name

Be joyful in You.

Psalm 5:11

<u>Joy</u>   Day 29

> **The LORD has done great things for us, And we are glad.**

Psalm 126:3

There are courses to help teenage drivers learn how alcohol affects and impairs their ability to drive. One strategy utilized requires the students to wear goggles that simulate impairment by blurring their vision. The students then attempt to drive golf carts around cones in a parking lot. Usually, the students knock over cone after cone. They do not realize how easy the course is to maneuver until they remove their goggles.

It is easy for us to have the same experience with God. There are times that our vision becomes blurred, and we fail to recognize the great things God has done for us. When our misplaced desires and concerns impair our vision, we may not see how blessed we are. Instead of recognizing and acknowledging all that we do have in our lives, we steal our own gladness. We choose to focus on what we do not have, could have, or what others have.

There are times that we may forget our own pasts and become blind to all that God has brought us through. Some complain about going to work on Monday and forget how they excitedly praised God when they first received that same job. Some disregard the loved ones God has placed in their lives and forget their times of past loneliness. At times, we may even submit to the discouragement of those who suggest that we have nothing to be glad about, even though we can clearly remember all that God has done us.

Let us strive to remove all that impairs our ability to see the great things God has done for us. Let us take stock of how good He has been in our lives. Let us seek to be glad.

Day 29

_____

_____

_____

_____

_____

_____

_____

_____

_____

_____

_____

_____

_____

<u>Joy</u>   Day 30

> *Oh, taste and see that the LORD is good; Blessed is the man who trusts in Him!*

Psalm 34:8

We are often told of various dishes that are pleasing to the tongue. We may hear of many fine cuisines. However, in order for us to know whether these treats truly are delicious to us, we have to personally try them for ourselves.

When we personally try God and sample the goodness that comes through Him, we can see for ourselves just how good He is. His goodness is not one that may appeal to some and be an acquired taste for others. Those who are willing to fully taste of the Lord want more of Him.

It has been said that "faith is the soul's taste."[5] Thus, when we apply our faith, have confidence in God, and allow the Lord to be more than just a flavor of the month, we will experience His goodness. Tasting the Lord's glory and revealing His goodness in our lives can encourage others to trust in Him, too. They may seek to personally know His joy for themselves.

Let us not listen to others who know of God's goodness. Let us have our our own personal confidence in Him and see His goodness in our own lives. Like a sweet dish, let us enjoy and freely tell others, "Hmmm . . . the Lord is good!"

---

[5] The Sword and the Trowel, "The Treasury of David." By Charles H. Spurgeon, 1885.

Day 30

_____

_____

_____

_____

_____

_____

_____

_____

_____

_____

_____

_____

_____

_____

_____

_____

_____

_____

Joy Day 31

Love does not delight in evil but rejoices with the truth.

1 Corinthians 13:6

A child custody battle between parents is a sad occasion to observe. Often, many good parents lose sight of and forsake what is best for their child(ren). These parents focus solely on the joy of winning their court case, even if it causes the other parent to have very little, if any, contact with their child(ren). Thankfully, everyone will not have the unfortunate experience of a custody dispute. However, a self-examination may reveal that we too may occasionally desire and rejoice in ungodly outcomes, instead of praying for a Godly result.

We may find joy in the pains and downfalls of someone who has committed wrongs against us or with whom we disagree. Some find guilty pleasure in gossiping about other's sins or in sharing the stories of their own past sins. Some rejoice because of injuries to individuals on a rival sports teams. As we get caught up in books, movies, and television programs, we may even find ourselves hoping for ungodly acts: such as pre-marital sex or adulterous relationships.

When we are led by the Spirit, we find joy in things that would bring joy to the Holy Spirit. What brings us joy reveals our true character. Let us have a character that is delighted with spiritual joy.

Day 31

_____

_____

_____

_____

_____

_____

_____

_____

_____

_____

_____

_____

_____

_____

_____

_____

_____

_____

_____

<u>Joy</u>   Day 32

> *Yet in all these things we are more than conquerors through Him who loved us.*

Romans 8:37

The legend of Robin Hood, also known as the Prince of Thieves, tells of how he stole from the rich to give to the poor. Today, we will not face the Merry Men of Sherwood Forest. We do, however, have encounters that threaten to steal and take away our joy.

Many people experience the loss of joy for reasons such as broken relationships, sickness, accidents, or a job loss. Indeed, sometimes the things that provide us with the most joy and fulfillment can quickly be gone. Therefore, while we enjoy our lives, let us also place our hopes on those things that are eternal.

When we lose our way and do not feel like moving on, let us turn to the one who will show us how to move forward. In sickness, let us turn to the one who gives courage and healing. When lonely, let us cling to the one who loves us eternally. Let us seek and find joy in our eternal Savior.

God does not have to take from anyone who is rich in joy to bless those who are poor is spirit. In fact, we have access to an abundance of joy in Him. With Him, we can overcome any obstacle. Because He is for us, nothing can stand against us. Through Him, we are not just conquerors. We are more!

Day 32

_____

_____

_____

_____

_____

_____

_____

_____

_____

_____

_____

_____

_____

_____

_____

_____

_____

_____

_____

<u>Joy</u>   Day 33

> *For I consider that the sufferings of this present time are not worthy to be compared with the glory which shall be revealed in us.*

Romans 8:18

There are so many areas of life in which we may choose to place our joy: personal accomplishments, family, relationships, finances, the life of or the hope of a child, etc. We may experience our greatest highs and joys from successes in these areas.   Unfortunately, we may also discover our deepest disappointments and lows from setbacks and failures in these very same areas of life. Occasionally, we face challenges so severe that all we once considered to be of the utmost importance begins to seem small. We feel that all we worked for has been lost forever.

During our struggles, let us never forget that we can experience true joy again. When we encounter dark clouds in our lives, let us not forget our eternal sun - the Son of God. Though our pain is real and will never be erased, our eternal Son is greater than our temporary sufferings. While we cherish and cling to our memories of who or what was lost, let us remember the eternal joy we will one day claim. When we express our humanity by way of our tears, let us not forget the glory that will be revealed to us through our faithfulness.

Let us show the world that in spite of our storms, we know there is still abundant joy through Christ. Let us reveal to the world that our joy is simply a fruit of the Holy Spirit living in us. Let us remember that the difficulty of our circumstances pales in comparison to the eternal joy awaiting us.

Day 33

_____

_____

_____

_____

_____

_____

_____

_____

_____

_____

_____

_____

_____

_____

_____

<u>Joy</u>   Day 34

> *These things I have spoken to you, that My joy may remain in you, and that your joy may be full.*

John 15:11

Isn't it great to know that we have a Savior who has promised that by remaining connected to Him, we will always have access to joy? In fact, as Jesus prepared the disciples for His crucifixion, He explained that He had shared His teachings with them so that they may be fruitful and have joy; not only that they have joy, but that their joy remain in them. Thus, during their dark times ahead, they could still be filled with joy.

We all experience ups and downs. There will be seasons for our highest successes and accomplishments. Likewise, there will be times when we encounter our darkest valleys. During our difficult periods, we may wish that we could have bottled up some of our prior joys for safekeeping until our moments of despair.

There are no real genies in bottles, but we do have access to the true joy that freely flows through Christ. He is more than a glass container that we break open in case of emergency. Through Christ, we can remain mindful of the eternal peace that awaits us. Through Him, we may faithfully cling to the knowledge of God's steady hand over our lives.

Let us be connected to Jesus as a branch to a vine and tap into the joy available through Him. Let us seek to have

His joy remain in us and to be filled by His joy. Then, no matter the circumstance we can proclaim, "I still have joy!"

Day 34

_____

_____

_____

_____

_____

_____

_____

_____

_____

_____

_____

_____

_____

_____

_____

_____

_____

<u>Joy</u>   Day 35

> *Now to Him who is able to keep you from stumbling,*
> *And to present you faultless Before the presence of His*
> *glory with exceeding joy,*

Jude 1:24

Personal disappointments and struggles come in all shapes and sizes. They may come in the form of unrealized hopes and dreams. They may be caused by those close to us and even by those who are simply associates. Our challenges may even be of our own creation. It is often at these times of disappointment that we seek God.

Trials will continue to come. We will always experience tests of our faithfulness, but God is always there to give us the strength to move past our obstacles. When we seek Him and His guidance, He can keep us from falling.

We may feel as though we cannot press forward. We may want to give up. Our fears and tears may tempt us to stop and to succumb to our circumstances, but we have a Father who is there no matter the difficulty or situation. He is able to keep us from falling.

Like a swimmer in distress, we can cause our rescue to be more difficult by trying too hard to save ourselves and preventing our rescuer from taking control. We may block our own blessings by refusing to let God take control. God is able to keep us from stumbling. Let us have joy in knowing that all we have to do is give in to Him and let Him guide us to where we can be presented with exceeding joy.

Day 35

_____

_____

_____

_____

_____

_____

_____

_____

_____

_____

_____

_____

_____

_____

_____

_____

_____

_____

Joy   Day 36

> *10 Create in me a clean heart, O God, And renew a steadfast spirit within me. 11 Do not cast me away from Your presence, And do not take Your Holy Spirit from me. 12 Restore to me the joy of Your salvation, And uphold me by Your generous Spirit.*

Psalm 51:10-12

Have you ever desired a fresh start? Have you yearned for the weight of certain burdens, struggles, and stains of secreted sin to be lifted? Have you longed for the scars of physical and emotional injuries that have been inflicted upon you to be cleansed and washed away? Whether because of actions that others have committed against us or that we have committed ourselves, we often wish to be freed from parts of our past or present.

In times like these, we wish for the trail that connects us to the past to be swept away. We want our spirits to be renewed with joy that will not expire. We seek the spiritual joy that comes from the salvation of God. Although we do not have the power to simply choose for joy to instantaneously fill our hearts, we can access our creator who can create a clean heart within us. He can fill us with the joy of His salvation.

The facts of our past may not change. The circumstances of our present may initially remain the same. However, holding close to and being filled by the joy of the Holy Spirit will give us a new, eternal perspective. With a new outlook, we can move forward toward changing our futures. Day by day, let us seek to separate ourselves from our past pains. Let us seek to be restored with His joy that is eternal.

Day 36

_____

_____

_____

_____

_____

_____

_____

_____

_____

_____

_____

_____

_____

_____

<u>Joy</u>   Day 37

> **Therefore by Him let us continually offer the sacrifice of praise to God, that is, the fruit of our lips, giving thanks to His name.**

Hebrews 13:15

When children are young, their parents often teach them to say, "Thank you." They want their children to learn to appreciate what is being done for them and not grow up with an attitude of expectation. Even though these simple words are taught as mere courtesies, it is hoped that a mindset and attitude of gratitude will follow.

Unfortunately, as adults, we sometimes forget this lesson ourselves. We forget to give thanks for the things God has done. We forget that although we may express joy with our lips by saying "Great" or "Thank God" to ourselves, we should still take time to give a prayer of thanks to Him.

If anything comes from our lips to reveal who we are, let it be praises to God. The fruit of our lips will show that we walk in the Spirit and understand more than mere courtesies and formalities. Let us give our thanks as an expression of our true appreciation and offer our thanks in the name of Jesus who died for us. Let us continually offer the sacrifice of praise to God, without the attitude that praise is a burdensome sacrifice.

Let us reveal the fruit of the Spirit in us through the joy that we regularly show through our continuous praise.

Day 37

_____

_____

_____

_____

_____

_____

_____

_____

_____

_____

_____

_____

_____

_____

_____

_____

_____

_____

_____

Love

Joy

Peace

Patience

Kindness

Goodness

Faithfulness

Gentleness

Self-control

CHAPTER 5

Peace

33 These things I have spoken to you, that in Me you may have peace. In the world you will have tribulation; but be of good cheer, I have overcome the world."

John 16:33

Peace   Day 38

> *And let the peace of God rule in your hearts, to which also you were called in one body; and be thankful.*

Colossians 3:15

Generally, a goal of technology is to provide greater comfort and ease to our lives. However, with more technological advances, it is easy to find ourselves becoming busier and busier. With all of our communication devices, we find ourselves always accessible and tempted to stay connected. Our minds stay focused on work or the next project for our family, work, or church. Eventually, many of us find that it is a struggle to have peace or to simply find time for rest.

A marvelous reward of focusing on and listening to the Spirit is that we can learn to allow the peace of God to rule in our hearts. No matter how busy we get, we can let God take control. When distractions come, peace may prevail. When challenges arise, peace rules. Though this may prove to be a lifelong lesson for many of us, it is great to know that we have access to peace in our daily comings and goings.

Let us listen to the voice of the Spirit and be guided to the peace of God that is always available to us. Let us receive Colossians 3:15 as a sincere directive. We may allow peace to prevail, if we only step aside and allow God to rule, not us.

Day 38

_____

_____

_____

_____

_____

_____

_____

_____

_____

_____

_____

_____

_____

_____

_____

_____

_____

_____

Peace   Day 39

> *Peace I leave with you, My peace I give to you; not as the world gives do I give to you. Let not your heart be troubled, neither let it be afraid.*

John 14:27

Before making large purchases like houses, vehicles, or even furniture, many people must acquire loans that must eventually be repaid. Likewise, when we want temporary access to many items, but do not wish to fully purchase them, we may have to rent them. It is typically only on special occasions like birthdays, anniversaries, and Christmas, that we receive free gifts without payment. How great to know that these are not the circumstances in which we access peace, which Christ freely left for us. Peace is always available to us.

On the night of His anticipated betrayal, Christ prepared His disciples for the challenges to come. He expressed to them that while He would not always physically be with them, His peace would remain with them. Thus, in the years ahead, through the disciples' challenges and difficult circumstances, the peace of Christ was available to them. All they had to do was receive it.

Let us learn that even before chaos and disappointment enter our lives, we already have access to peace. The world adds conditions when giving anything away, but Christ left us with an unconditional and eternal peace. The only condition we have is to allow Him into our hearts. Let us learn that a piece of Christ is the key to our peace.

Day 39

_____

_____

_____

_____

_____

_____

_____

_____

_____

_____

_____

_____

_____

_____

_____

_____

_____

_____

<u>Peace</u>   Day 40

> **Finally, brethren, whatever things are true, whatever things are noble, whatever things are just, whatever things are pure, whatever things are lovely, whatever things are of good report, if there is any virtue and if there is anything praiseworthy—meditate on these things.**

Philippians 4:8

It is easy to become distracted and lose sight of God's ways. The world gives us so many alternative messages that we may easily lose focus. Instead of focusing on Him, the world says that it is all about us. In the world, we are told to focus on our pleasure, our money, our materials, or simply to accept popular culture, even if it goes against God's Word.

When we evaluate whether our lives are focused on the right things, we can simply ask, "Is there any *virtue*?" Are our actions *noble* and *just* or self-serving? Do we act in *truth* and *purity* or lie in order to get what we want? Are our actions worthy of *good report* or tales of secret sins? Do we seek those things *lovely* and pleasing to God and meditate on them for guidance?

Let us focus our thoughts on Godly ambitions and have our minds set on where God wants us to be. He has a unique path and plan for each of us that is both to His glory and for our good. Let us not miss out on the opportunities He places before us. Let us stay focused and meditate on Him and His ways.

Day 40

_____

_____

_____

_____

_____

_____

_____

_____

_____

_____

_____

_____

_____

_____

_____

_____

_____

_____

_____

Peace

> *11 Not that I speak in regard to need, for I have learned in whatever state I am, to be content: 12 I know how to be abased, and I know how to abound. Everywhere and in all things I have learned both to be full and to be hungry, both to abound and to suffer need.*

Philippians 4:11-12

There is much excitement in watching children learn to crawl, walk, speak, and accomplish so many other firsts. We understand that a child will not learn to speak a first word one week and then sing the ABC's the next week. Even as adults, it often takes us years to learn new skills and facts. However, many of us become frustrated as we struggle to immediately find peace when encountering life's challenges. We want instant results.

Paul wrote about his own struggle with this process in his letter to the Philippians and explained that he had to learn to be content. It was not a spontaneous event in which he attained grand maturity and everlasting peace. He learned how to be content through a process. We, too, can break away from expectations of immediate contentment.

In our fast paced culture where instant gratification is the norm, let us accept that we must learn contentment. In Christ, we may find peace from challenge to challenge and from success to success. Through Christ, let us learn how to be steady and unmovable during our ups and downs. We can do all things through Christ who gives us strength.[6]

---

[6] Philippians 4:13

Day 41

_____

_____

_____

_____

_____

_____

_____

_____

_____

_____

_____

_____

_____

_____

_____

_____

_____

_____

Peace   Day 42

> **God is our refuge and strength, A very present help in trouble.**

Psalm 46:1

There are times when all that we truly desire is to just take a break and rest. We want time to refuel our minds and emotions from all the busy hours of life. We may feel physically tired because we have not taken time to rest because of all we have to do. At times, we may feel broken down due to the emotional mountains we have climbed and from the heart aches we have endured.

When we have these moments, it is good for us to go to our place of refuge and to our source of strength. Whether in a time of trouble or in a time of spiritual, physical, mental, or emotional exhaustion, we have God as a continuous refueling station. The issue, though, is how do we access and utilize this source.

We should not wait and only turn to God during our times of trouble, for we can regularly go to Him. Let us take time to be with God daily so that we do not feel as if we must go and search for Him. Instead of seeking Him, we can have a relationship in which we can simply turn to Him and find our refuge.

Day 42

_____

_____

_____

_____

_____

_____

_____

_____

_____

_____

_____

_____

_____

_____

_____

_____

_____

> *29 Take My yoke upon you and learn from Me, for I am gentle and lowly in heart, and you will find rest for your souls. 30 For My yoke is easy and My burden is light.*

Matthew 11:29-30

With the common usage of tractors, it is rare to see mules or oxen connected with a yoke around their necks, pulling a farmer along in a field. However, for many, this is the image that comes to mind when considering committing their life to Christ. They equate the Christian life with carrying a heavy load that will steal their joy and tell them everything in their life is wrong. Unfortunately, this idea is often relayed to them by Christians, who seem to only speak of gloom in their own personal lives.

Jesus explains that while He indeed is a yoke that one may assume, He is far from a heavy burden. His yoke is easy. In fact, He operates opposite of the traditional yoke. Instead of adding weight, He takes the weight of our burdens. Instead of restraining us, He strengthens us in times of trouble and propels us forward. All we have to do is volunteer, and we will discover Him to be the key to peace.

Let us choose to submit to a yoke that does not confine us but only serves to keep us closely connected to Christ. When we are near Him, we can give our burdens to Him, knowing that He will never leave nor forsake us. With Christ, we may be chained to eternal peace.

Day 43

_____

_____

_____

_____

_____

_____

_____

_____

_____

_____

_____

_____

_____

_____

_____

_____

_____

Peace Day 44

> *¹ I will lift up my eyes to the hills— From whence comes my help? ² My help comes from the LORD, Who made heaven and earth. ³ He will not allow your foot to be moved; He who keeps you will not slumber.*

Psalm 121:1-3

During our lowest moments or when seeking strength to face challenges, we choose how we will respond to our emotions. Just as "beauty is in the eye of the beholder," we have the opportunity to choose how we will perceive and respond to mountains in our lives. Do we focus on the challenging terrain that can discourage us and weigh down our hearts, or do we set our eyes to where we may find strength?

Let us fix our eyes on God. The creator of heaven and Earth is more powerful and grander than any trial or situation that we may encounter. We may be shaken by our temporary problems, but He is a timeless God. He is a God who was, is, and will be. Therefore, we do not have to worry about how to deal with tomorrow. He will be with us then, just as He is now.

Whether in the valleys of our situations or down on our knees with nowhere to look but up, let us choose to gaze upon our higher power and not on our challenges. When we focus on God, we discover that He is taller and higher than any mountain we will ever face.

Day 44

_____

_____

_____

_____

_____

_____

_____

_____

_____

_____

_____

_____

_____

_____

_____

_____

_____

Peace   Day 45

> [38] *But He was in the stern, asleep on a pillow. And they awoke Him and said to Him, "Teacher, do You not care that we are perishing?"* [39] *Then He arose and rebuked the wind, and said to the sea, "Peace, be still!" And the wind ceased and there was a great calm.* [40] *But He said to them, "Why are you so fearful? How is it that you have no faith?"*

Mark 4:38-40

As a storm approaches, dark and threatening clouds can be seen drawing near. Trees sway from the strengthening winds. The sound of thunder booms in the distance. There is the scent of the coming rain. We feel the first heavy drops of rain. With all of these signs, we know to seek shelter. For with proper shelter, we can have peace that we will endure the coming storm.

Like storms in the weather, we all experience storms in our lives. These storms may come from different directions, have multiple causes, and have various possible outcomes. Yet, there is still one common shelter available to us for peace, Jesus. In Christ, we have a reassuring lover whose guidance can lead us through our most difficult times.

Just as one songwriter wrote, let us proclaim, "Though the storms keep on raging in my life . . . my soul is anchored in the Lord."[7] Let us not be fearful like the disciples who were physically present with Christ. Let us have peace in

---

[7] Douglass Miller, *My Soul Has Been Anchored* (Living On Top 1990).

knowing He is always with us, no matter our circumstances.

Day 45

_____

_____

_____

_____

_____

_____

_____

_____

_____

_____

_____

_____

_____

_____

_____

_____

<u>Peace</u>   Day 46

> *¹ The Lord is my shepherd; I shall not want. ² He makes me to lie down in green pastures; He leads me beside the still waters. ³ He restores my soul; He leads me in the paths of righteousness For His name's sake. ⁴Yea, though I walk through the valley of the shadow of death, I will fear no evil; For You are with me; Your rod and Your staff, they comfort me. ⁵ You prepare a table before me in the presence of my enemies; You anoint my head with oil; My cup runs over. ⁶ Surely goodness and mercy shall follow me All the days of my life; And I will dwell in the house of the Lord Forever*

Psalm 23:1-6

The Twenty-third Psalm has been read and memorized for generations. Its power is obvious, even though it only consists of merely six verses. The Psalm also is an indicator of our need for comfort. Through each generation, this Psalm has reminded us that peace is available to us because of who and how our God is. He is a God who can grant us peace by covering our needs.

Just from the verbs of the scripture, we learn how He cares for us. God *makes* us *lie* down in green pastures, *leads* us, *restores* our souls, *comforts* us, *prepares* a table before us, and *anoints* us. And He does all this while He *"is"* with us. Meanwhile, all that is left for us is to choose not to fear the shadows of difficulty and simply let Him have our cups run over with His blessings. By doing this, His goodness and mercy will *follow* us for life.

Let us choose to follow our great Shepherd. Let us look for the ways He exists with us. Let us take the time to understand that through our various situations and positions in life, He can guide us. No matter our circumstances (even when we put ourselves in bad situations), we eventually may find peace if we follow our Shepherd.

Day 46

_____

_____

_____

_____

_____

_____

_____

_____

_____

_____

_____

_____

_____

Love

Joy

Peace

Patience

Kindness

Goodness

Faithfulness

Gentleness

Self-control

CHAPTER 6

Patience

Wait on the LORD;

Be of good courage,

And He shall strengthen your heart;

Wait, I say, on the LORD!

Psalm 27:14

Patience   Day 47

> **But those who wait on the LORD Shall renew their strength; They shall mount up with wings like eagles, They shall run and not be weary, They shall walk and not faint.**

Isaiah 40:31

In elementary school, we are taught that a verb is a word of action. The verb "wait" does not invoke the idea of progress or action. It is important, however, to note that the act of waiting requires a specific choice with a specific outcome intended. Just as someone actively runs to a predetermined destination, waiting also suggests an expected result.

When we wait on the Lord, we show that we are not casually loitering and looking to see if there will be some coincidental encounter. Either we wait on the Lord knowing that He will arrive and take action in our lives, or we simply go through the motions. Praying in times of trouble just because we were taught to do so, but without any true expectation for God to impact our circumstances, is only looking - not waiting. Waiting is trusting and believing.

We have been promised that though we may be tired, our strength will be renewed with faithful waiting. Let us continue to wait for God in our circumstances and wait for the day of Christ's return. Let us wait with confidence that our ticket to eternity has been purchased. Instead of going through the motions, let us wait with assurance that our trip to heaven is only a matter of time.

Day 47

_____

_____

_____

_____

_____

_____

_____

_____

_____

_____

_____

_____

_____

_____

_____

_____

_____

Patience   Day 48

Therefore be patient, brethren, until the coming of the Lord. See how the farmer waits for the precious fruit of the earth, waiting patiently for it until it receives the early and latter rain.

James 5:7

Each of us experiences various seasons in our lives, more than just the four seasons of the calendar year. These seasons may sometimes last for years. We have seasons of joy and new blessings, periods of brokenness, times of recovery, etc. Throughout these experiences, our commitment and willingness to wait on the Lord may vary. We may even have seasons in how passionate we are for God, as we deal with the circumstances we are encountering.

During the seasons of our lives, we have the example of farmers to guide us. Farmers do not always see the desired amount of sun or rain come each day, but they still wait for their crops to grow. They faithfully wait to reap the crops that they have faithfully sown throughout the season.

Let us learn to have patience through our seasons and circumstances. Let us have confidence in waiting on our crop, through the sun and rain of life. Let us not lose hope or lose our passion for Christ. Rather, let us wait patiently on Him, for one day we will reap and receive the crop of eternity. Let us not just trust God only for a season, but throughout our lives.

Day 48

Patience   Day 49

Love suffers long . . .

1 Corinthians 13:4

Many believers long to live a Spirit-guided life. They also understand that they should do so through love, the first fruit of the Spirit listed. However, in our fast-paced society, where there is pressure to respond quickly, many Christians fail in Paul's very first description of love, long-suffering or patient.

When we truly express spiritual love, it is not selfish, material, or lustful. It is an active representation of God's love for us. In suffering long with love, we learn to forgive multiple times, just as God patiently forgives us over and over again. We care enough to overcome being quick-tempered, just as God does not retaliate against us. We long to better communicate our love through means that may be better received. We accept being patient, not only with family and spouses, but with our enemies and neighbors.

Longsuffering does not mean to endure abuse in order to love. We must protect ourselves from abuse (domestic, verbal, sexual, etc.), for we cannot love others if we have not learned to love ourselves. So, let us be careful not to cause others to feel abused from our lack of patience or force others to suffer in their attempts to love us. Let us act out our love with patience and be constant in our efforts to love. Let us not fail to love.

Day 49

_____

_____

_____

_____

_____

_____

_____

_____

_____

_____

_____

_____

_____

_____

_____

_____

_____

_____

Patience   Day 50

> *Be anxious for nothing, but in everything by prayer*
> *and supplication, with thanksgiving, let your requests*
> *be made known to God;*

Philippians 4:6

Many children believe that they can drive cars the same as their parents. It does not matter that they cannot touch the pedals or even see over the steering wheel yet. In the eyes of these children, they are fully prepared to take on the task of driving. Likewise, many of us prematurely aspire to immediately attain certain status levels. We desire to have particular possessions or positions. We seek to assume new responsibilities professionally or in the body of Christ. Some eagerly await to marry. The reality, though, is that the time is not right because we are not prepared.

Instead of looking to an artificial timeline or comparisons with others, we can perform a spiritual evaluation to know whether it is time to step forward in faith. There is a difference between being obedient to the will of God and being anxious to promote our own will. So, let us pray for the opportunities to be prepared, and then, wait patiently to grow.

Like a child growing to see over the steering wheel, God will be a booster for us when it is time to move forward. Like teenagers waiting to become licensed, God will give us maturity to proceed, but we must have patience. For without His boost and guiding wisdom, we are more vulnerable to wreckage, struggles, and failures that could be avoided with patience.

Day 50

_____

_____

_____

_____

_____

_____

_____

_____

_____

_____

_____

_____

_____

_____

_____

<u>Patience</u>   Day 51

> [2] *My brethren, count it all joy when you fall into various trials,* [3] *knowing that the testing of your faith produces patience.*

James 1:2-3

It is commonly stated at graduation ceremonies that the value of an education is something that can never be taken away. One comedian noted, that as a child, he believed this meant that even a thief could not break into a house and steal a diploma. However, it is not the certificate that holds this special value, but the doors that are opened because of the experience and knowledge acquired to attain the degree.

Just as there are tests and trials in school, we too face personal challenges in our lives. Like we did in school, we have the opportunity to learn from our successes and our mistakes. We may also learn that using patience helps us to successfully pass our present and future trials. Throughout all of this, we have the bible as a text book that can guide us.

We never know when we will encounter the next pop quiz in life. So, we must be patient during our personal tests and have joy in knowing that we will eventually graduate to a higher level. Let us patiently store up the lessons learned from our trials as we prepare to face the journeys ahead.

Day 51

_____

_____

_____

_____

_____

_____

_____

_____

_____

_____

_____

_____

_____

_____

_____

_____

_____

_____

_____

_____

Patience   Day 52

Therefore we also, since we are surrounded by so great a cloud of witnesses, let us lay aside every weight, and the sin which so easily ensnares us, and let us run with endurance the race that is set before us,

Hebrews 12:1

Hebrews 11 covers centuries of momentous occasions in just one chapter. This chapter is well-known for its recounting of how faith played a role in the actions of so many different individuals. We may be tempted to believe that God performed those types of acts then, but not anymore. It may seem that miracles no longer occur in our modern times. Instead, we should recognize that the Almighty God of the past is the same God of the present. God still works miracles every day.

Today, when we face our challenges, we can either give up or patiently endure until God acts. Distractions and disbelief may momentarily hold us back. We choose, however, whether to give up or to push them aside and move forward. Temptations and personal weaknesses will cling to us, yet if we hold onto God, we may stay free from their grasp.

When in need of a miracle, let us endure and know that our powerful God will not give us more than we can bear with Him. No matter the race before us, God is with us. Since He is with us, let us patiently wait and allow Him to act and perform miracles in our lives.

Day 52

_____

_____

_____

_____

_____

_____

_____

_____

_____

_____

_____

_____

_____

_____

_____

_____

_____

_____

> *Now we exhort you, brethren, warn those who are*
> *unruly, comfort the fainthearted, uphold the weak, be*
> *patient with all.*

1 Thessalonians 5:14

Has anyone ever annoyed you? This is often described as getting on someone's nerves. Has there been someone whose mannerisms and actions aggravated you such that you did not want to be in their presence? Some people are easily bothered by those who regularly misbehave. Others become frustrated with those who are negatively considered whiny, and who complain about handling the smallest of tasks.

We may encounter people like this in our families, jobs, and churches. Often, the temptation or practice is to avoid any potential encounters with them in order to keep our own positive mindset or so that we do not disturb our own day. However, when we choose to display the patience of the Spirit, we may find constructive ways to interact with those who we once avoided.

Although we may not be able to completely adjust the behavior of others, we may be able help others face their own issues when we strive to patiently be more like Christ. Through being patient with others, we may learn that the reason for their behavior is actually a cry for help. We may even come to recognize just how often others have regularly been patient with us. Let us allow others to experience the love of Christ through our patience.

Day 53

Patience   Day 54

> *But seek first the kingdom of God and His*
> *righteousness, and all these things shall be added to*
> *you.*

Matthew 6:33

There is virtue in preparation and planning. In fact, the Boy Scout motto is "Be prepared." It is easy, however, for us to become so focused on our plans that our preparation grows from preparedness to preoccupation to worry. It is easy to spend our time on and waste our emotional energy with concerns for what we should do, could do, or what might happen next. Thankfully, Jesus has given us a simple system for preparation with two active steps: 1) seek the kingdom of God and 2) seek God's righteousness.

Seeking is not something we do passively. Seeking is an action we do with purpose. When we actively seek the kingdom of God first, we are forced to prioritize. When we are intentional about seeking God's righteousness, we are forced to evaluate our priorities. In fact, through seeking God's righteousness, we may discover that our plans and preparations need to change. Suddenly, the things that concerned us the most may seem less significant, when looked upon with a Godly-kingdom perspective.

Through purposely seeking God and His righteousness, we can learn not to focus on the things that are important according to the world. Instead, we learn to be patient, while God works to provide all that we need according to His plan.

Day 54

_____

_____

_____

_____

_____

_____

_____

_____

_____

_____

_____

_____

_____

_____

_____

_____

_____

_____

<u>Patience</u>   Day 55

> *For I know the thoughts that I think toward you, says the LORD, thoughts of peace and not of evil, to give you a future and a hope.*

Jeremiah 29:11

When reading a book, there is sometimes the temptation to flip ahead to the climax to find out what happens in the end. Now that viewers have access to entire seasons of television shows on DVD or by the internet, there also may be the temptation to skip episodes to see how the season ends. Sometimes, we wish to take sneak peeks ahead in our own lives because even though we trust God, we are still concerned with what lies ahead in the future.

Jeremiah 29:11 reminds us that no matter the situation, circumstance, or trial, the Lord's thoughts toward us are not of evil, but of peace. No matter what we experience, He has given us a future and a hope. Our future and hope may not always be what we desire. In fact, it may be difficult, at times, to be patient and faithful beyond our immediate circumstances.

Let us not forget that our immediate circumstances and eternal reality are not separate. As with Job, when we turn the pages of our lives to the final chapter, God's thoughts to us are of ultimate and eternal peace. Let us work to excel at revealing the fruit of patience. Let us have an eternal view of each individual day, with patience.

Day 55

_____

_____

_____

_____

_____

_____

_____

_____

_____

_____

_____

_____

_____

_____

_____

_____

_____

_____

_____

Love

Joy

Peace

Patience

Kindness

Goodness

Faithfulness

Gentleness

Self-control

CHAPTER 7

Kindness

[37] "Then the righteous will answer Him, saying, 'Lord, when did we see You hungry and feed You, or thirsty and give You drink? [38] When did we see You a stranger and take You in, or naked and clothe You? [39] Or when did we see You sick, or in prison, and come to You?' [40] And the King will answer and say to them, 'Assuredly, I say to you, inasmuch as you did it to one of the least of these My brethren, you did it to Me.

Matthew 25:37-40

Kindness   Day 56

> *But love your enemies, do good, and lend, hoping for nothing in return; and your reward will be great, and you will be sons of the Most High. For He is kind to the unthankful and evil.*

Luke 6:35

We are no longer under the law of the Old Testament. We are freed by grace, through Christ. Now, we live by the Spirit. One way of showing that we are of the Spirit is by showing that we have the character traits of God. This can be done by revealing the fruit of kindness to all, just as God has done for us all - even though none of us is deserving.

Luke 6:35 identifies certain ways in which we show kindness. For some, it may be easy to grasp the concept of loving our enemies. Many recognize the significance of performing good deeds. Some of us even have no problem lending. Christ issues a challenge, however, in this scripture by telling us to not even hope for anything in return.

If we desire to have the traits of God, our kindness should not be contingent upon whether we will be thanked. When we reveal the fruit of the Spirit in us, we do not evaluate if the recipient of our kindness has earned it. No matter if others are unthankful or even evil, our kindness should indicate that we are focused on the ultimate reward – being considered children of the Most High God. We show that we are the children of the Most High God by acting like it, with kindness.

Day 56

_____

_____

_____

_____

_____

_____

_____

_____

_____

_____

_____

_____

_____

_____

_____

_____

_____

_____

<u>Kindness</u>   Day 57

> *Do not let kindness and truth leave you; Bind them around your neck, Write them on the table of your heart,*

Proverbs 3:3

In Nathaniel Hawthorne's book, *The Scarlet Letter*,[8] the character Hester Prynne is forced to wear the letter "A" on her chest as a symbol of her sin of adultery. Today, instead of intentionally wearing symbols that report personal sin, it is common to see people wearing symbols associated with faith. However, a fish symbol on a car, a cross on a necklace, or even a cross as a tattoo does not reveal a person's true character or commitment to God. Our true commitment to God is not something that is evident in jewelry or markings. It is recognized in our fruit and character.

Physical markings and jewelry can be taken off or removed. One act of kindness may be forgotten or overshadowed by countless other acts of selfishness or rudeness. To continuously reveal the trait kindness, we need to make it a part of our character and who we are. When we are bound to kindness like chains, we will be kind regardless of when it is, where we are, or whether we feel like it.

Let us spiritually secure ourselves with kindness and truth such that it never leaves us. Like the tablets where

---

[8] Hawthorne, Nathaniel. *The Scarlet Letter.* Boston: Ticknor, Reed & Fields, 1850

scripture was written and passed down from generation to generation, let us write kindness and truth on our hearts so that it will not fade from day to day.

Day 57

_____

_____

_____

_____

_____

_____

_____

_____

_____

_____

_____

_____

_____

_____

_____

_____

Kindness

Love . . .is kind

1 Corinthians 13:4

Just as wealth may be passed from generation to generation, so may family values and lessons. These lessons, once learned or adopted by others in the past, in time, may prove to be either valid or not. Nevertheless, such lessons, along with the opinions of our associates, may cause us to instinctively respond in certain ways towards certain people and situations. The question may ultimately be asked, are we guided by the values of others or the value of love taught by Christ?

Do we have a litmus test for when we will be proactive with kindness? Do we criticize the unwed mother and forget that she chose life over abortion? Do we avoid helping the young people in particular neighborhoods because we think their community should help their own? Do we refuse to assist some individuals due to the differences in our political opinions and miss out on opportunities to share the gospel? At first sight, such unkindness may give others a false view of true Christianity.

Let us not discriminate in our love, but kindly love all. We are to love our neighbors and enemies as ourselves. We are not at war with our neighbors. We should not need a diplomatic policy to establish how to actively be kind to others. We need a spiritual policy of love that motivates us to act with kindness.

Day 58

_____

_____

_____

_____

_____

_____

_____

_____

_____

_____

_____

_____

_____

_____

_____

_____

_____

_____

Kindness

> [4] *God our Savior showed us how good and kind he is.* [5] *He saved us because of his mercy, and not because of any good things that we have done, but according to His mercy He saved us, through the washing of regeneration and renewing of the Holy Spirit,*

Titus 3:4-5

We have access to so many comforts by way of modernization or our citizenship that it is easy to feel entitled to certain comforts and luxuries. However, if we attempt to believe that we are entitled to salvation, then just when did we earn God's grace and mercy? What act has anyone ever done that caused him or her to be entitled to eternal life? How did they earn the forgiveness of their sins and wrongdoings? What words have ever been spoken that entitled someone to the mercy of God?

Truly, there is no action that we can take or word we can ever speak that will prove that we deserve God's mercy. Even though we could never earn mercy, Christ died for us as the ultimate act of kindness. If God never does anything else for us, His kindness (by way of His grace and mercy) truly is sufficient.

Let us show that we do not take grace for granted. We can show that we do appreciate His loving kindness toward us through our kindness to others. As Christ has been kind to us, let us express to the world that we, as God's children, have this spirit of kindness.

Day 59

_____

_____

_____

_____

_____

_____

_____

_____

_____

_____

_____

_____

_____

_____

_____

_____

_____

_____

_____

Kindness   Day 60

> *He who oppresses the poor reproaches his Maker, But he who honors Him has mercy on the needy.*

Proverbs 14:31

We strive most days to improve ourselves, our financial security, and our position in life. Along the way, there may be the temptation to look down on or discount those who are not making the same strides that we are making. It is easy to impose our own experiences, expectations, and backgrounds onto their situations. We may ask why has he or she chosen to remain in or give in to that lifestyle. We may wonder what mistakes have they made to cause them to struggle or to be in their circumstances.

Instead of examining for fault in the lives of others, let us seek ways that we can bless others. While we are taking time to criticize, we may be failing to recognize the opportunities God has provided for us to help others. We may be missing chances to share knowledge that God has blessed us to have. How many families and children might be impacted if we stopped sharing opinions and started sharing time? We may need to take the time and ask, "Where would we be if there was not a blessing in our past or in the past of our families long ago?"

To honor our God is to honor His ways. So, let us honor Him in how we treat others. This day, let us have mercy on those in need. Let us seek to serve others with a spirit of kindness, knowing the mercy and grace God has shown toward us.

_____   **Day 60**

_____

_____

_____

_____

_____

_____

_____

_____

_____

_____

_____

_____

_____

_____

_____

_____

_____

Kindness   Day 61

> *Judge not, and you shall not be judged. Condemn not, and you shall not be condemned. Forgive, and you will be forgiven.*

Luke 6:37

During courtroom trials, a verdict is not given until all the evidence has been presented. Only then does a judge or jury make a decision about the case. Away from court, it has become common for opinions and critiques to be made about a person based on individual acts or associations. How would we appear if God treated us based on a moment's glance during our past failures or times of weakness? If we were to be judged based on our fruit, we would hope that the decision would not be made until we were fully ripe.

Our acts or attitudes of kindness to others should not focus on the temporary or former circumstances. Our kindness should have a long term and eternal view. This view allows us to be kind regardless of the moment.

We can choose to be kind regardless of someone's past acts or current situations. Our kindness should never condone what is wrong. However, we should never forget the grace that God abundantly provides.

Let us be mindful that our momentary acts of kindness may be the God-sent, spiritual inspiration someone needs to grow closer to Him. While we continue to grow ourselves, let us be careful in what we say to others or about others. We all need forgiveness. So, let us treat others with a kindness that reflects the grace God has given each of us.

Day 61

_____

_____

_____

_____

_____

_____

_____

_____

_____

_____

_____

_____

_____

_____

_____

Kindness   Day 62

> ***Therefore, whatever you want men to do to you, do
> also to them, for this is the Law and the Prophets.***

Matthew 7:12

So many people have become familiar with "The
Golden Rule" that some do not attribute it to being one of
Christ's teachings. Now, some even use a twisted version of
Christ's teaching as an excuse to treat others harshly and to
have a defensive mindset. They offer, "I will treat others
badly if they cross me because I would expect the same in
return."

For us to follow Jesus' teachings, we must do more than
just go through the motions of kindness. We must move
beyond simply performing one individual kind act and
waiting for the right time to perform another. We should
move toward having an ongoing attitude of kindness.
Charitable donations and being courteous are ways of
showing kindness. Our hearts, however, may reveal whether
our motivations were to show a spirit of kindness, to make
impressions on others, or for a tax deduction.

Are your thoughts toward others thoughts of kindness or
self-promotion? Do you have a pure heart of kindness, or are
you simply displaying well-trained public behaviors? Do you
manifest the pure kindness of the Spirit in your thoughts and
actions? If so, there will be fruit. Let us seek pure hearts that
reveal the attitude we want others to have with us.

Day 62

_____

_____

_____

_____

_____

_____

_____

_____

_____

_____

_____

_____

_____

_____

_____

_____

_____

_____

_____

<u>Kindness</u>   Day 63

> *But a certain Samaritan, as he journeyed, came where he was. And when he saw him, he had compassion.*

Luke 10:33

Living by the Spirit and being kind are not qualities that will be noticed at first sight. Kindness is a fruit that is revealed in our actions. A kind heart actively shows kindness without reservation or hesitation. Whereas patience is responsive, kindness is not passive or awaiting an invitation. Kindness takes initiative. The parable of "The Good Samaritan" exemplifies such initiative.

The priest and Levite both crossed the street when they saw the man in need. Their actions moved them away from showing kindness. Had they known the man's full background, perhaps they would have stopped to help. However, it was the "kind" Samaritan who showed initiative and stepped into action. He acted without concern for who would be the recipient of his kindness. He did not know the story of the man in need. He simply acted.

Let us not be conservative, but liberal in our loving kindness. Let us be like the Samaritan who had compassion at first sight. He did not dwell on lessons passed down through generations. He simply saw someone in need and acted with compassion. Let us work to have hearts of kindness that seek opportunities to serve, no matter the recipient.

Day 63

_____

_____

_____

_____

_____

_____

_____

_____

_____

_____

_____

_____

_____

_____

_____

_____

_____

_____

_____

_____

Kindness   Day 64

> *Give, and it will be given to you: good measure, pressed down, shaken together, and running over will be put into your bosom. For with the same measure that you use, it will be measured back to you.*

Luke 6:38

In the movie *Pay It Forward*,[9] a young boy creates a national phenomenon with a simple idea - do kindness to others without expectation of something in return, and eventually, it could come back to bless you. Instead of blindly paying it forward with kindness, today, many believers and non-believers prefer to withhold their kindness until there is certainty that there will be reciprocity.

When it comes to kindness, it does not matter if we have material wealth to share. Though we may be accustomed to associating scriptures about giving in reference to tithes and offerings, there are more ways to give other than financially. Regardless of our present financial status, there are ways we all can give. When we possess so much kindness that it overflows when shared, we give as Christ tells us to give.

Let us focus on making an investment of kindness. A return on this type of investment is promised. It may not be immediate or when we first desire it, but God is never late.

---

[9] *Pay It Forward*, Dir. Mimi Leder. Warner Brothers Entertainment, Inc., 2000. Film.

Let us be mindful that active kindness is a resource we all have. The more resources we have, the more we can kindly share. No matter if it is our time, knowledge, food, patience, experiences, etc., let us use the resources we have and *"pay it forward."*

Day 64

_____

_____

_____

_____

_____

_____

_____

_____

_____

_____

_____

_____

_____

_____

_____

Love

Joy

Peace

Patience

Kindness

Goodness

Faithfulness

Gentleness

Self-control

CHAPTER 8

Goodness

⁸ He has shown you, O man, what is good;

And what does the LORD require of you

But to do justly,

To love mercy,

And to walk humbly with your God?

Micah 6:8

Goodness   Day 65

> *And whatever you do in word or deed, do all in the name of the Lord Jesus, giving thanks to God the Father through Him.*

Colossians 3:17

There are various professions in which someone is appointed to speak on behalf of some other person or business. Whether as an agent, lawyer, or spokesperson, the job requires spreading a particular message or idea for another. In each case, the performance of the person hired may lead to positive or negative impressions about who or what they are representing. Likewise, we often form our opinions about certain people or companies based on our interactions with their agents or representatives. This may be for better or for worse.

Those who have not accepted Christ but know of our faith in Him, may look to us to gather an understanding of what Christianity is really about in practice. As His representatives, we have grand opportunities to make statements about His goodness. We can easily do this through the goodness of our words and deeds.

What impression would others have about God based on your actions? When you have the opportunity to reveal the fruit of the spirit in your words and deeds, what are you showing? Are you working to be a representative of Jesus?

Whatever we say or do, let us try to reveal the goodness of Jesus in us. We never know who is watching!

Day 65

_____

_____

_____

_____

_____

_____

_____

_____

_____

_____

_____

_____

_____

_____

_____

_____

_____

_____

_____

_____

_____

_____

Goodness   Day 66

> **Let your light so shine before men, that they may see your good works and glorify your Father in heaven.**

Matthew 5:16

Businesses are often successful when there is the presence of at least two components: 1) a good product or service and 2) good marketing or advertising to inform others about the business. As believers, we should be about Christ's business. Nothing can top the service he provided that made forgiveness and salvation available to all. So, we should serve as living commercials, advertising how we have been blessed and how He is available to all.

When we let the light of Christ in us shine, we broadcast to all the gift of His love and grace. Too often, we try to lead others to Christ by revealing their sins and personal darkness without revealing to them the light and love of Christ. Jesus tells us here in Matthew 5:16, that when we let our light shine, others will see Christ's goodness for themselves.

Let us live our lives in such a way that we regularly promote Christ. Let us give others free samples of the goodness that is associated with Christ. When we are walking models of His joy and show His light by our good works, we glorify our Father in Heaven.

Day 66

_____

_____

_____

_____

_____

_____

_____

_____

_____

_____

_____

_____

_____

_____

_____

_____

_____

_____

_____

_____

_____

_____

Goodness   Day 67

Love . . . thinks no evil;

1 Corinthians 13:5

In loving others, there is often the fear of becoming vulnerable to emotional hurts and disappointments. When we are hurt, there is then the tendency to say, "I will forgive, but I will not forget." Some people even offer that it is not possible to control what we think, and thus, impossible to forget. So, why even pretend to forgive.

We may not be responsible for what others do to us or for the actions that take place around us. We are, however, responsible for how we choose to respond to situations. Therefore, let us choose to respond, in love, with acts of goodness. Let us not waist time considering potentially negative circumstances that *might* never even occur. Let us avoid spending emotional energy on how we *might* respond to defend ourselves against those who *might* upset us. Instead, we can focus on the good that *will* come when we respond positively with good works and love.

Proverbs 23:7 reads "For as he thinketh in his heart, so is he." Whether at work, in relationships, or in parenting, we can choose to not dwell on evil, but on goodness. How blessed are we, that God loves us so much that He does not think evil towards us for all we have done in the past. So, let us reflect his goodness in our thoughts and deeds.

Day 67

Goodness   Day 68

> **Woe to you, scribes and Pharisees, hypocrites! For you pay tithe of mint and anise and cummin, and have neglected the weightier matters of the law: justice and mercy and faith. These you ought to have done, without leaving the others undone.**

Matthew 23:23

Each year, countless people vow to lose weight. They buy exercise equipment or videos that promise a body makeover. They see commercials with testimonials from people who say they have used certain fitness programs and had extreme results. Many people eventually purchase the equipment or videos expecting certain results, but fail to accept a key component to success - the diet. One can exercise regularly, but junk food each day will prevent the progress desired.

Believers often face a similar test. We learn outward actions to act like followers of Christ, yet we fail to care for the more important matters of the soul. We may have traditional religious activities and conversations like the scribes and Pharisees did. However, unless we commit our hearts to the weightier matters of Christ's teachings exemplified through the fruit of the Spirit, we cannot reach a higher place in Christ.

So, let us work to purge ourselves of the activities, mindsets and things that prevent of from growing stronger in Christ. Let us subscribe to a diet that produces a closer walk with Christ. Instead of only seeking the outward results that others can see, let us seek a makeover from the inside out. Then, our good works will reveal our spiritual fitness.

Day 68

Goodness   Day 69

> **17 But whoever has this world's goods, and sees his brother in need, and shuts up his heart from him, how does the love of God abide in him?**

1 John 3:17

Panhandlers can often be found in most large cities. They commonly hold signs asking for money or food. Upon seeing these signs, each of us has decided whether to roll down our car windows and contribute to a cause that we may have a legitimate reason to question. There are other times when we will learn of those who have a particular need and are not broadcasting their situation for all to know. Yet, because assisting them may inconvenience us more than simply rolling down our window, we refuse to help.

Are we afraid to leave our comfort zones to do good for others? Do we cling to our privacy and refuse to offer a bed or couch to a family for more than a one night stay? Do we care so much for our schedule such that we refuse to provide someone with a ride so that (s)he may get to work and in order to care for his/her family? Some who are unable to bear children may feel led by God to adopt, but refuse because it is not the way they desired to have children.

Let us not only desire to do good for others, but let us seek out the ways to do so. The opportunity to act may not always present itself as someone holding a sign underneath a flashing light. It may be posted in an expression on a solemn face waiting for us to ask if we can help. Let us show that the love of God abides in us, through our good works.

Day 69

_____

_____

_____

_____

_____

_____

_____

_____

_____

_____

_____

_____

_____

_____

_____

_____

_____

Goodness   Day 70

> *For we are His workmanship, created in Christ Jesus for good works, which God prepared beforehand that we should walk in them.*

Ephesians 2:10

Pastor Rick Warren's book, *The Purpose Driven Life,*[10] aided readers in understanding God's visions for their lives. The book detailed how we are to love God, love others, and live a life pleasing to God. While Pastor Warren provided a detailed and contemporary guide to living a life of purpose, Paul wrote about it succinctly in his letter to the Ephesians.

Paul's letter reminds us that a creator has an intended purpose in mind for His creations. Our creator allowed for us to be saved by grace for His good works. While we may find personal pleasure and enjoyment with our eyes, ears, tongues, and limbs, these are not the purposes of our lives in Christ. As His workmanship, we should walk in the path He has laid before us - to serve Him by serving others.

Let us be thankful for grace. Let us find the good works to which we can and will commit ourselves. By serving others, we may serve God. Through fellowship with others, let us worship God. Let us always remember, who we are and whose we are.

---

[10] See note 3.

Day 70

_____

_____

_____

_____

_____

_____

_____

_____

_____

_____

_____

_____

_____

_____

_____

_____

_____

Goodness   Day 71

> *And do not be conformed to this world, but be transformed by the renewing of your mind, that you may prove what is that good and acceptable and perfect will of God.*

Romans 12:2

Just like the peer pressure experienced by teenagers trying to find their identity, Christians also find themselves challenged with how to adapt to an ever-changing world. Do we allow our opinions on issues to change or shift away from God's teachings? Do we conform to the ways of the world? Do we seek our answers about present day issues from our eternal God or from shifting public perceptions on temporary issues?

Instead of changing who we are as Christians in order to avoid discomfort when we differ with those of the world, let us find our comfort in God. He will renew our minds so that we may stay focused on Him and His ways. By being transformed from the world's standards to His standards, we can reveal to the world what is the proper way of God, whether the world agrees or not.

Yes, we have free will. Yes, we have the freedom to engage in various activities according to our laws, even when we know the acts are sinful. However, let us not be misguided by what the world finds acceptable.

We have a heavenly master who reveals to us what is

spiritually and eternally proper. Let us be transformed to the standards of God's Word, and not conform to the ways of this world. Let us stand on His Word and have confidence in "what is good and acceptable and [the] perfect will of God."

Day 71

_____

_____

_____

_____

_____

_____

_____

_____

_____

_____

_____

_____

_____

_____

_____

Goodness   Day 72

> *And let us not grow weary while doing good, for in due season we shall reap if we do not lose heart.*

Galatians 6:9

Though often overlooked, farming is a necessary component of any economy. No matter the economic situation, there is always a need for food. Farmers are occasionally forced to re-evaluate their dedication and commitment to farming when encountering seasons of drought, flooding, and ever-changing costs of fertilizer and produce. Yet, they proceed with dedication and the belief that in time, they will see the benefits of their planted crop.

As believers, we too face questions of whether to continue living lives that are pleasing and honorable to God. Our culture grows more toward being self-focused, seeking immediate pleasure, and satisfying indulgences. So, it can become easy for us to abandon our efforts of goodness to others if there is no immediate gratification in return. Without immediate rewards, it is easy to forget about doing good and to simply focus on ourselves. However, just as the dedicated farmer, we too should have faith that we will reap what we have sown.

Let us not be concerned with being rewarded for our good works. Our due season may be soon, or it may not come until we reach eternity. Nevertheless, let us continue to show the light of Christ in us and through our good works. Let us remember that our eternal reward will be immensely greater than any we could ever receive now.

Day 72

_____

_____

_____

_____

_____

_____

_____

_____

_____

_____

_____

_____

_____

_____

_____

_____

_____

_____

_____

_____

<u>Goodness</u>   Day 73

Blessed are the pure in heart, For they shall see God.

Matthew 5:8

What is more pure than the love of God, in sending Christ to die for us so that we may have eternal life, with Him? For this and more, we all want to be with God. In Matthew 5:8, Jesus shared that those who are pure in heart "shall see God."

Purity is not the direct result of strict adherence to religious traditions and practices. A pure heart is not evidenced by speaking in such a way that everyone who hears us knows we are Christians. Commitment to such things, without more, was the way of the Pharisees who Jesus called white washed tombs.

The act of purposely drawing closer to God is more than a religious routine or custom that has been passed down through generations. Let us not allow such things to get in the way of our genuine fellowship with God. When we focus on fellowship with God, we can grow to becoming more like Christ.

We do not have to declare how often we pray or for how long we study God's word each day. It is not about the quantity. It is the quality of our study and fellowship that is important. Let us work and ask God to establish pure hearts within us.

Day 73

_____

_____

_____

_____

_____

_____

_____

_____

_____

_____

_____

_____

_____

_____

_____

_____

_____

_____

Love

Joy

Peace

Patience

Kindness

Goodness

Faithfulness

Gentleness

Self-control

CHAPTER 9

Faithfulness

[14] What does it profit, my brethren, if someone says he has faith but does not have works? Can faith save him? [15] If a brother or sister is naked and destitute of daily food, [16] and one of you says to them, "Depart in peace, be warmed and filled," but you do not give them the things which are needed for the body, what does it profit? [17] Thus also faith by itself, if it does not have works, is dead.

James 2:14-17

Faithfulness   Day 74

For we walk by faith, not by sight.

2 Corinthians 5:7

Runners may repeat a saying or mantra to themselves in times when they become tired and seek motivation to reach the end of their race. Many Christians also utilize this strategy with scripture when encountering challenging times in life. Proverbs 3:5 is one such scripture. It reminds us that the Lord has the answer to our situation and will see us through.

Even though we have learned and know to trust in God, we may still exclude God from our thinking on a regular basis. We choose not to lean on Him. Instead, we rely on our personal knowledge and understanding for answers to our difficult problems, without even considering God's will. This is not an exercise of faith or trust. This is not leaning on God.

The act of leaning requires us to be off balance and unsteady. It requires that we acknowledge that someone or something is strong enough to support and stabilize us. We can be fully stable when we are wholeheartedly committed to leaning on and trusting in the support God. By being faithful, we learn to lean on Him.

Our own understanding may provide theories about our situations, our lives, and even our creation. However, trusting in God with a whole heart gives us a firm foundation that is more than a theory. Trusting in God is what occurs when we are faithful and seek Him to direct our paths. Let us reveal to the world that we are full of faith by being faithful.

Day 74

_____

_____

_____

_____

_____

_____

_____

_____

_____

_____

_____

_____

_____

_____

_____

_____

<u>Faithfulness</u>   Day 75

> ***Trust in the LORD with all your heart, And lean not on your own understanding.***

Proverbs 3:5

In the movie *Indiana Jones and the Last Crusade,*[11] Indiana Jones, played by Harrison Ford, must pass a series of tests on his way to finding the Holy Grail. One test required that he step out over an abyss with no bridge and no visible way of crossing. The key to passing required stepping out with the faith that he would be able to successfully make it over, regardless of what he saw.

We, too, may have times when we cannot see how we will pass our current test or circumstances, but faithfully we press onward. We may endure for days or for years, with nothing left to hold on to except our faith. We may be tempted to give up on God and His promises. Some choose to trust only in what they know or can personally see. It is the act of walking by faith, however, that will guide us through our temporary circumstances toward our final destination.

Let us understand that there are times when being blinded by faith is the only way to see clearly. No matter if the circumstances were created over the course of days or years, let us have faith in our God whose power extends

---

[11] *Indiana Jones and The Last Crusade*. Dir. Steven Spielberg. Paramount Pictures, 1989. Film.

across eternity. Faith can serve as our compass, whether we are lost or simply trying to make sure we are on course. Let us walk by that faith.

Day 75

_____

_____

_____

_____

_____

_____

_____

_____

_____

_____

_____

_____

_____

_____

_____

Faithfulness   Day 76

> **Love ... ⁷ bears all things, believes all things, hopes all things, endures all things. ⁸ Love never fails.**

1 Corinthians 13:7-8

Jesus tells us to love without conditions. Our society dictates, however, that we reciprocate at certain times and under certain conditions. We are told that if we believe our love has not been accepted the way we want, we are entitled to move on and away.

Fairy tales would have us believe our love should be reserved for one soul mate, specifically placed on the planet as the perfect match for us. In fact, there has only been one person to walk this planet who has shown us perfect and faithful love - Jesus. It is His love that serves as an example of how we should be faithful to God by loving others.

He is faithful and committed to us. His love for us bears all, in spite of the times that we have been uncommitted to Him. His love endures all, even when we have placed other things and people ahead of our relationship with God. Though we have these times of being unfaithful, He is still there.

Embracing God's love teaches us how to move past the temporary and shallow standard of love promoted in our culture. Through Him, not only do we learn to love more than those close to us. We learn to never cease in loving all. Let us continue to faithfully cling to the Word and express love that endures.

Day 76

_____

_____

_____

_____

_____

_____

_____

_____

_____

_____

_____

_____

_____

_____

_____

_____

Faithfulness   Day 77

That if you confess with your mouth the Lord Jesus and believe in your heart that God has raised Him from the dead, you will be saved.

Romans 10:9

Children often repeat the familiar refrain, "sticks and stones may break my bones, but words will never hurt me." As they grow older, they eventually learn how false this statement is. They learn that words do indeed have power to love, injure, destroy, and also to create. The power of words can also be used in revealing the fruit of the Holy Spirit living in us. For when we use our words to reveal our faithfulness, we have access to the power of saving grace.

In 1919, A.B. Kendall described how "it takes only a few brief words to enter the married life; but . . . We enter the Christian life by faith in Christ and by confessing Him as Lord and Master of our lives."[12] Our faithfulness and the sincerity of our confessions is typically evidenced by a life of commitment. However, it all begins with a simple admission.

Let us be unafraid to admit that Jesus is Lord. Let us have confidence in sharing our faith in the completeness of God as Father, Son, and Holy Spirit. Let us be willing to show the fruit of our faith in our faithfulness to Him and His Word.

---

[12] A.B. Kendall, "Confessing and Denying Christ" in *The Herald of Gospel Liberty* (July, 1919), 20.

Day 77

_____

_____

_____

_____

_____

_____

_____

_____

_____

_____

_____

_____

_____

_____

_____

_____

_____

_____

_____

_____

Faithfulness   Day 78

But without faith it is impossible to please Him, for he who comes to God must believe that He is, and that He is a rewarder of those who diligently seek Him.

Hebrews 11:6

Some soap operas have storylines in which children are entitled to inheritances, but no one knows that a particular individual is actually an heir. Often, it is a long kept secret, or the person dying does not even know. This heir may be someone who lives in the same community and is already known by all of the characters on the television program. Thus, it is not the presence of the heir that grants them the inheritance, but recognition of the heir's identity that grants them the right to the inheritance.

To be heirs of God, let us not only acknowledge that there is a God. Let us recognize the almighty nature of God; that *He is* God the Father, Son, and Holy Spirit; that *He is* the beginning and end; that *He is* creator of all. In understanding who *He is*, we understand that *He is* the great **I am**, who through grace, rewards salvation to those who find Him. Let us have faith in who *He is* and identify ourselves as His children.

Countless people say they believe in a higher power, but fail to embrace God. We have been blessed because God allowed us to find Him and to know Him. So, let us take time to learn more about Him, better understand who *He is*, and be faithful to Him. Let us recognize that *we are* children of God. Let us identify ourselves as His heirs.

Day 78

_____

_____

_____

_____

_____

_____

_____

_____

_____

_____

_____

_____

_____

_____

_____

_____

_____

_____

_____

_____

<u>Faithfulness</u>   Day 79

> **⁴⁷ Most assuredly, I say to you, he who believes in Me has everlasting life. ⁴⁸ I am the bread of life.**

John 6:47-48

At some point in time, most of us have become familiar with the association of cause and effect. For instance, if we do not eat, it will cause us to feel hungry. If we do not rest, we will become weary and tired. As we grow in our Christian walk, we come to learn and experience spiritual cause and effect, as well. Jesus told us that because we believe in Him, the effect is that we have eternal life.

Some believers create or add additional procedures or theological obstacles that must be conquered before someone receives salvation and eternal life. Christ tells us, however, that it is a pure spiritual diet of Him that is necessary. Our physical bodies need nutrition, but we need faith in Christ, the bread of life, for our eternal health.

Let us partake of the bread of life and begin our eternal lives now, in the present, because of our faithfulness. Our physical forms will eventually perish. Although, with faith we are just beginning to live! Let us live faithfully such that others may see our faithfulness as a fruit of the Spirit in us.

Day 79

_____

_____

_____

_____

_____

_____

_____

_____

_____

_____

_____

_____

_____

_____

_____

_____

_____

> ***Thus also faith by itself, if it does not have works, is dead.***

James 2:17

Parents of a child just born into the world anxiously await the sound of crying to know that their child lives. A car without gas or a charged battery lacks the sound of a roaring engine if the car is not prepared to travel. Likewise, true faith is evidenced by our faithfulness to God and the fruit we produce.

Evidence of our faithfulness to God is not what is seen in our appearance or adherence to specific religious traditions, for there are many traditions spread across many denominations of Christianity, who all share the same faith and belief. Likewise, acknowledging the existence of God alone is not evidence of faithfulness. Even those who choose to follow witchcraft and satanic practices may believe in God.[13] However, it is the application of our faith that separates us and reveals our belief.

Let us uncover the faith within our hearts by our actions. Let us allow the light of our faith to shine bright. Just as the prophecy of the Messiah was fulfilled in the life and works of Christ, let us reveal our faithfulness by following the Messiah's teachings.

---

[13] James 2:19

Day 80

_____

_____

_____

_____

_____

_____

_____

_____

_____

_____

_____

_____

_____

_____

_____

_____

_____

_____

_____

Faithfulness   Day 81

> *Above all, taking the shield of faith with which you will*
> *be able to quench all the fiery darts of the wicked one.*

Ephesians 6:16

There are types of insurance for almost every aspect of life: home, auto, health, life, flood, fire, pet, etc. The list goes on. One count identified at least 85 different types of insurance.[14] How great it would be if we had insurance to help us bounce back from our personal struggles? Wouldn't it be nice to have insurance when we are flooded by temptation or struck by the symptoms of sin? Actually, we do have insurance - faith.

When our hopes are destroyed, faith in our redeemer restores us. When disappointments or the death of loved ones impede into our lives, faith renews our spirit. When ideas contrary to the Word of God are planted around us, faith can repel lies and implant the truth. While insurance is there in the event that tragedy occurs, faith in God prepares us and stands with us even before tragedy is conceived.

We do not, however, need to pay a premium for our insurance. Christ paid the price for all. Our faith is free, and the benefits are eternal. Let us not only have faith, but be faithful and utilize the great shield of faith that cannot be penetrated.

---

[14] "Category: Types of Insurance" Wikipedia, The Free Encyclopedia. Wikimedia Foundation, Inc. 27 September 2013. Web. 11 Dec. 2013. (Ranging from Alien Abduction Insurance to a Zombie Fund)

_____   **Day 81**

_____

_____

_____

_____

_____

_____

_____

_____

_____

_____

_____

_____

_____

_____

_____

_____

_____

<u>Faithfulness</u>   Day 82

Whenever I am afraid, I will trust in You. I will trust in You.

Psalm 56:3

Author Neale Donald Walsch writes that F.E.A.R. is really False Evidence Appearing Real.[15] We can apply our own lives as examples of how true this acronym actually is. How many times have we backed away from opportunity because we were afraid of failure? How many times have we chosen not to act because of reasons that were not realistic or likely? How many times have we not stepped out on faith because of the mere possibilities of what might happen?

When we are afraid, we have a God in whom we can trust. He has a proven track record. The true evidence of God's presence in our lives shows that we have no reason to fear or to be afraid. The same God who has the power to create life and heal a weakened body has the power to work through our circumstances.

Let us place our trust in God and not in our doubts, emotions, or human nature. It is human to be afraid, but we reveal the fruit of the supernatural Spirit when we learn to trust God in spite of our circumstances. Let us allow our fruit to reveal our faithfulness.

---

[15] Walsch, Neale Donald. *Neale Donald Walsch on Relationships*. Hampton Roads Publishing: 1999. Print.

Day 82

_____

_____

_____

_____

_____

_____

_____

_____

_____

_____

_____

_____

_____

_____

_____

_____

_____

_____

Love

Joy

Peace

Patience

Kindness

Goodness

Faithfulness

Gentleness

Self-control

CHAPTER 10

Gentleness

4 Whosoever therefore shall humble himself as this little child, the same is greatest in the kingdom of heaven.

Matthew 18:4

Gentleness   Day 83

if My people who are called by My name will humble themselves, and pray and seek My face, and turn from their wicked ways, then I will hear from heaven, and will forgive their sin and heal their land.

2 Chronicles 7:14

In chemistry, there are formulas. For manuals, there are instructions. In cooking, there are recipes. God also has provided a prescription to help His children guide the world away from sin. Instead of blaming sinners and passing judgment on the lives and lifestyles of others, we can follow God's instructions from 2 Chronicles 7:14. There He provided steps to bring order to a broken nation.

When we pray and seek God's face, we are on the way to changing our world. When we turn from our misguided ways and to a Godly path, we can help others facing their troubles. God is only waiting to heal our land. However, the first step written in the scripture may be the most difficult, for we must first humble ourselves.

It may take time for us to learn how to **humble** ourselves before God. It may take time for us to shake away the shackles of pride, but we can learn to **pray to, seek for, turn toward, and hear from** God. The time has come for us to set the stage for God to heal our land. So, let us voluntarily humble ourselves before He allows us to be humbled.

Day 83

_____

_____

_____

_____

_____

_____

_____

_____

_____

_____

_____

_____

_____

_____

_____

_____

_____

_____

_____

Gentleness   Day 84

> ²³ *for all have sinned and fall short of the glory of God, ²⁴ being justified freely by His grace through the redemption that is in Christ Jesus,*

Romans 3:23-24

Where do you live? Where do you work? Where did you go to school? These questions are typical parts of conversations between people meeting for the first time. For some, it is a casual way of getting to know one another. Although, for others, it may serve as a means of comparing lives and distinguishing a status.

Do I earn more than you? Is my neighborhood more elite than yours? Is my church bigger or more prestigious than yours? Though it may not always be through these standards, we often seek ways to compare ourselves to others.

Romans 3:23-24 provides the ultimate equalizer. We all have sinned. We all fall short of God's glory. It is only through Christ that we are redeemed. It does not matter who we are or who our family may be. Our past or current lifestyles do not matter. We have no reason to elevate ourselves above others nor do we have any excuse to diminish our own value. The same price was paid for us all, and the richest person could never afford to pay it.

Let us never give in to temptation to feel low or exalted by ourselves to others. Let us not become "holier than thou" or "lower than thou" Christians. We do not know what God has done in someone else's life. What we can be sure of, is that even though we all have sinned, Christ's sacrifice has paid the way for us all.

Day 84

_____

_____

_____

_____

_____

_____

_____

_____

_____

_____

_____

_____

_____

_____

> [4] *... Love does not envy; love does not parade itself, is not puffed up; [5] does not behave rudely, does not seek its own ...*

1 Corinthians 13:4-5

On average, there are more mirrors in a home than there are bibles. In fact, most people spend more time looking into mirrors each day than spending time in fellowship with God. While this reality may reveal the emphasis our culture places on appearances and de-emphasizes God, it too may reflect the emphasis we place on "I" and "me." When it comes to loving others, however, we must learn to lessen the emphasis on "us" and increase the emphasis on "how" God would have us love others – with a humble heart.

Pure love does not seek its own or focus attention on itself. Loving others with a humble heart requires that we separate our personal desires from the blessings of others. This love is expressed as a verb, just like the act of feeding.

Someone feeding a child or weaker adult is not envious of what is being eaten. The goal is simply to assure that the other person receives the food. Likewise, let us love without concern for our own increase. Instead of being rude or envious because someone else receives a blessing (healing, house, position, spouse, child, etc.) that we also wanted, let us be satisfied with knowing that he or she has been blessed.

Let us learn to love without the focus always being on us. Let us focus on the love of Christ. He loved us so much that He gave up His own life that we might receive the great gift of eternal life.

Day 85

_____

_____

_____

_____

_____

_____

_____

_____

_____

_____

_____

_____

_____

_____

Gentleness   Day 86

> *But the wisdom that is from above is first pure, then peaceable, gentle, willing to yield, full of mercy and good fruits, without partiality and without hypocrisy.*

James 3:17

When conversing with others, we usually do not understand what someone else is expressing to us solely based on the words that are being spoken. Often, it is not what is said, but also how something is said that communicates the meaning. Indeed, changing the emphasis on a word or altering the inflection of our voice can convert our words from expressing love to being sarcastic or angry.

Throughout the bible, we learn that how we speak may reveal godly wisdom, and wisdom may reveal our humility. Psalm 37:5 informs us that "The words of a wise man's mouth are gracious." Proverbs 11:2 instructs us that "with the humble is wisdom." James 3:17 further explains that godly wisdom also will be revealed in our gentleness. It is by traits such as purity, a willingness to yield, and being merciful that we expose our godly wisdom. None of which is fully possible to embrace without God's help.

Like Solomon's prayer for knowledge in 1 Kings 4:12, let us seek wisdom to better serve God. Let us pray to be peaceful, pure, and to display other traits of gentleness described by James. Let us desire to have hearts and minds filled with wisdom from God, not just knowledge from the world. With Godly knowledge, we can reveal to others the true nature of God. We can do so not only by what we say, but by how we say it and show it in our gentleness.

_____   **Day 86**

_____

_____

_____

_____

_____

_____

_____

_____

_____

_____

_____

_____

_____

_____

_____

_____

_____

<u>Gentleness</u>   Day 87

> *Be humble when you correct people who oppose you.*
> *Maybe God will lead them to turn to him and learn the*
> *truth.*

CEV

2 Timothy 2:25

There are certain people who are commonly referred to as "Know it Alls." No matter the subject, they seem to have an answer for everything and want you to know just how smart they are. Eventually, those who are around them avoid asking questions or just avoid being in their presence, even if Mr. or Mrs. Know It All is often correct.

We run the risk of doing this in our efforts to spread the Word. Although we do not want to condone sin or the world's ways, we must be careful how we wield our swords of truth. In our attempts to cut others free from the chains of bondage and sin, we may find ourselves piercing them such that they refuse to give Christ a chance. If all that is felt when encountering Christians is the pain of correction, the world will never learn to accept the healing love of Christ.

We must learn to be passionate, yet gentle, in sharing how great God is. We should be gentle in explaining what He asks from us. In 2 Timothy 2:25, we see that though we may provide an example of humility, it is God who turns people to the truth, not us. Let us do as President Theodore Roosevelt stated, "Walk softly and carry a big stick." The

Word of God is both the biggest and gentlest of all.

Day 87

_____

_____

_____

_____

_____

_____

_____

_____

_____

_____

_____

_____

_____

_____

_____

_____

_____

_____

_____

<u>Gentleness</u>   Day 88

> *For the LORD takes pleasure in His people; He will beautify the humble with salvation.*

Psalm 149:4

There are countless ways that our relationship with God may be disrupted. For example, a lifestyle centered on impressing others can lead us on a path away from God. This may be more than being focused on materials such as cars, houses, clothes, shoes, etc. We may be intent on telling others about all we have done, the things we have purchased, or places where we have traveled. Nevertheless, our primary concern is not what God knows of our hearts but the thoughts others have of us. Thus, it is important that we conduct an occasional self-evaluation of our priorities.

Do we acknowledge that God is Lord over us? Do we aim to walk humbly? Unlike Jesus, we are imperfect. So, we will fail from time to time, *but GOD* takes pleasure in His people. In fact, he has preserved salvation for those who humble themselves to Him.

When we continue to acknowledge Him as the Lord of lords, we humble ourselves. When we humble ourselves to God, we will not be concerned with the impressions that others have of us. We will focus on God's standards. If we do consider the thoughts of others, let others see that we serve and follow our Almighty God.

Day 88

_____

_____

_____

_____

_____

_____

_____

_____

_____

_____

_____

_____

_____

_____

_____

_____

_____

Gentleness   Day 89

> **Assuredly, I say to you, unless you are converted and become as little children, you will by no means enter the kingdom of heaven.**

Matthew 18:3

Children mature from depending on their caretakers to wanting their independence; from believing all that they are told (from Santa Clause to the Tooth Fairy) to questioning everything; and from being sincere and genuine to having pride. In fact, younger children seemingly hide their wrongdoings due to fear of punishment, not because of pride. Pride tends to come with age and maturity.

To adopt a heavenly mindset, we must unlearn some lessons and convert back to how we began as young children. We may not be punished for refusing to be humble. God may allow us, however, to encounter experiences that allow our pride to be reduced.

Pride in things such as our wealth, positions, or God given talents may be counterbalanced by our personal struggles in those same areas. Some struggles may be due to our arrogance about our accomplishments or from over-valuing ourselves. With such a mindset, childlike humility may occasionally be forced upon us.

With each passing day, let us learn to resemble the genuine nature of a child. Let us seek God. Let us accept that there is a Holy Father greater than us all. Instead of seeking verification of our value, let us seek to enter the kingdom of heaven.

Day 89

_____

_____

_____

_____

_____

_____

_____

_____

_____

_____

_____

_____

_____

_____

_____

_____

Gentleness   Day 90

> **When pride comes, then comes shame; But with the humble is wisdom.**

Proverbs 11:2

We have seen it time and time again. Pastors, politicians, business leaders, and athletes have all publicly fallen. At one moment, they reach or are on the way to accomplishing new personal heights. Next, the results of their sin and its shameful results are revealed. These failings, however, are not limited to public figures. We all have encountered it or experienced it on our own levels.

During our successes, it is important to remember that God has blessed us with our gifts, opportunities, or prosperity. Just as Satan tempted Jesus, we also will be tested. However, we can turn our temptations and tests into a testament about God's role in our lives. Having humility like Jesus will allow us to listen and receive Godly wisdom to overcome our trials. When we are humble, we move beyond paying too much attention to ourselves. Instead, we recognize how to serve others.

No matter how proud we feel of any act we have done, nothing can compare to the sacrifice of Christ that excels all others. Christ is the model of humility. He is the only one who has ever saved the eternal lives of all humanity - dead, living, and yet to live. Let us wise up to the power of God, humble ourselves, and acknowledge His power over our lives. Let us accept that it is better to be humble than to be humbled.

_____ **Day 90**

_____

_____

_____

_____

_____

_____

_____

_____

_____

_____

_____

_____

_____

_____

_____

_____

_____

Gentleness   Day 91

> *¹⁰ That at the name of Jesus every knee should bow, of things in heaven, and things in earth, and things under the earth ¹¹ And that every tongue should confess that Jesus Christ is Lord, to the glory of God the Father.*

Philippians 2:10-11

Societies and cultures have a tendency of categorizing people, attributing a particular value to a person's status, and classifying an importance on peoples' lives. It is seen in our media when someone considered to have a high status experiences a tragedy. There is more attention given to that person's situation than when the same event occurs in the life of someone less known. We see this done by income, communities, schools, occupations, group affiliations, etc. There implicitly seems to be a public focus on who should be considered relevant or not.

No matter how others view our status, let us recognize that our social circles are not of ultimate consequence. Our temporary and artificial hierarchies do not really matter. There is only One who is and will always be number one, and we all have access to Him. It is "at the name of Jesus that every knee shall bow."

Just as we know that He is superior, let us also acknowledge that His ways are superior, as well. If the Son of God was humble and gentle, then we have no reason to exalt ourselves above others. The risen Savior died for all of us.

So, let us accept that at this moment, we are just as important in the eternal kingdom as any other person on Earth. Likewise, let us also recognize that everyone else is just as important as we are. No matter anyone's status, wealth, or who they know, we all have an equal right to salvation through Christ.

Day 91

Love

Joy

Peace

Patience

Kindness

Goodness

Faithfulness

Gentleness

Self-control

CHAPTER 11

Self-Control

[8] This book of the law shall not depart out of thy mouth; but thou shalt meditate therein day and night, that thou mayest observe to do according to all that is written therein: for then thou shalt make thy way prosperous, and then thou shalt have good success.

Joshua 1:8

<u>Self-Control</u>   Day 92

> *16 I say then: Walk in the Spirit, and you shall not fulfill the lust of the flesh. 17 For the flesh lusts against the Spirit, and the Spirit against the flesh; and these are contrary to one another, so that you do not do the things that you wish.*

Galatians 5:16-17

From September of 1971 to February 1984, a child named David Vetter suffered from a rare genetic disease that left him unusually vulnerable to illnesses. In order to prevent sickness, his bedroom was converted into a sterilized, plastic chamber that was created to protect him from harm. He commonly became referred to as a "Bubble Boy."

Few have ever lived in sterile, physical conditions like David Vetter. We all, however, must learn to avoid infectious temptations that threaten our spiritual health. Paul writes that for protection, we can submit to the bubble of the Holy Spirit.

When we walk in the Spirit, our thoughts are guided by those things that are spiritually pure and not just physically satisfying. The Holy Spirit will direct us away from the impulsive directions where our flesh lusts to go. Outside the bubble of the Spirit, we become more vulnerable to the fleshly temptations of our emotions, bodies, and pride.

Let us walk in the Spirit wherever we go. The Spirit is more than a plastic bubble. The Spirit is not limited to a building or a particular room. So, not only can we walk in the Spirit, we can work, drive, and fellowship, all while we choose to find our rest in the Spirit's bubble.

_____   **Day 92**
_____

_____

_____

_____

_____

_____

_____

_____

_____

_____

_____

_____

_____

_____

_____

_____

_____

Self-Control   Day 93

> *For God has not given us a spirit of fear, but of power and of love and of a sound mind.*

2 Timothy 1:7

When we focus on our pasts, we all have numerous examples of failure and times that we have missed our mark. However, we are not alone. The bible is essentially a collection of failures and defeats that were eventually overcome through faithfulness to God. Our past shortcomings occasionally may dissuade us from even attempting a new challenge. We fear yet another defeat. Though we do not doubt God's power, the weight of our doubt and fear prevents us from moving toward our next victory.

Isn't it great to know that God's fruit to us is not a spirit of fear? He has given us a spirit of power. He has given us a spirit of love. He has given us a spirit of a sound mind.

A mindset and spirit of power will allow us to have confidence in the midst of our challenges. The spirit of love in our hearts will keep us gentle towards others as we overcome barriers. A sound mind will keep us focused on the authority of God over our lives.

When we have daily time with God, we can refocus on His power and not on our past weaknesses. Through time with Him, we may control our fears and walk with a sound mind, in love, and with power. Through prayer and by meditating on Him, we can tap into these resources that God has given us and maintain our focus each day.

_____

_____

Day 93

_____

_____

_____

_____

_____

_____

_____

_____

_____

_____

_____

_____

_____

_____

_____

_____

_____

Love . . . is not provoked,

1 Corinthians 13:5

What some describe as love causes many people to react in a variety of ways. Some are positively motivated by love to care for others, to strive through difficult circumstances, and to endure all types of challenges. Meanwhile, others react according to their pride, vulnerabilities, or desire for control. Ultimately, they reveal their lack of self-control. Their emotions lead them astray such that they quickly become jealous, violent, or easily provoked.

Love that is easily provoked is love in theory, not love in practice. Being easily provoked reveals that we are not motivated by a love for others. It shows that we are simply using love as an excuse and tool to get what we want and to primarily make ourselves happy, even if we must force others along. However, when we are not easily provoked, we can slow down and reveal that love is a consistent state of being, not just a behavior we engage in from time to time.

With self-control, we learn how to respond to each situation instead of just reacting. We take the time to respond to others with a loving state of mind and with loving attitudes. When love is our true motivation, we eventually learn to react with a pure, self-controlled love.

Let us commit ourselves to learning love as an instinctive reaction, when we might otherwise be provoked.

With self-control, we can learn to love continuously, rather than just performing individual nice acts. God's constant reaction to us is love. Let us exercise self-control and be more like Him.

Day 94

_____

_____

_____

_____

_____

_____

_____

_____

_____

_____

_____

_____

_____

_____

_____

_____

<u>Self-Control</u>   Day 95

> ***Your word I have hidden in my heart, That I might not
> sin against You.***

Psalm 119:11

There are many outward signs that may suggest
someone has faith in God. Many people carry their bible into
church services but never open the bible or read it when not
at church. It is common to see people in public wearing
necklaces with a cross or crucifix. Some people customarily
tell others to "have a blessed day." However, none of these
surface expressions or actions require or guarantee that
someone has received Christ into his or her heart.

Applying God's Word in our lives is what reveals that
we have received Him into our hearts - not things like acting,
speaking, or dressing religiously. We should do more than
just appear to have access to God's Word. Let us consume
and internalize His Word.

Possessing food does not prevent hunger. Having water
available does not make someone immune to thirst. It is by
consuming, eating, or drinking that we are satisfied and
fulfilled. So, let us receive His Word into our hearts.

Let us tap into Him as the source of our self-control, so
that we do not sin against Him. Let us become intimate with
his Word such that it resonates within us and is revealed as
the fruit of self-control. In order to have His Word, we must
take time to read and receive His words. Let us protect His
Word within us, apply it, and live by it.

Day 95

_____

_____

_____

_____

_____

_____

_____

_____

_____

_____

_____

_____

_____

_____

_____

_____

_____

_____

Self-Control   Day 96

Do you not know that you are the temple of God and that the Spirit of God dwells in you?

1 Corinthians 3:16

The Holy temple of Jerusalem was built and rebuilt during the time of the Old Testament. It was the central place for the worship of God. It was tended to with strict rules and with special attention given to every detail. There were also strict rules utilized in offering sacrifices to atone for sins.

Now, because of Christ, there is no longer a need to make sacrifices in order for our sins to be forgiven. We do not even require a physical building in order to worship or fellowship with God. Each of us is now a temple of God. However, do we treat ourselves with the care worthy of a temple of God?

Do we take the time to care for our temples spiritually or physically? Do we expose our temples to the filth of lust and sin in what we view and read? Do we abuse our temples with alcohol, drugs, or even food?

Let us not be careless with our temples. Whether physically weak or strong, it is the temple of God. Let us spiritually empower our temples regularly with fuel. Instead of being like the Israelites who built but had to rebuild the temple because of carelessness and unfaithfulness, let us remain faithful and controlled with our temples.

Day 96

_____

_____

_____

_____

_____

_____

_____

_____

_____

_____

_____

_____

_____

_____

_____

_____

_____

_____

_____

<u>Self-Control</u>   Day 97

> *For to be carnally minded is death, but to be spiritually minded is life and peace.*

Romans 8:6

The power of addiction is an enemy that many people battle throughout their lives. Addiction is not restricted to substances such as illegal drugs and alcohol. There are countless addicts of shopping, eating, sodas, prescription drugs, internet sites, etc. These addicts find momentary peace and solace in their addictions. Some try to move away from their addictions, but struggle to find peace outside of the dead end nature of their habit. Ultimately, they usually face the inevitable consequences of their actions.

For many of us, it is not a clinically recognized dependence that we face. It is the power of compulsions like anger, impatience, peer approval, and financial irresponsibility that serve as our albatross. No matter who we are, we all fight against the addictions of our flesh and carnal minds.

A key step in Alcoholics Anonymous is the recognition that there is a greater power. As believers in Christ, our primary tool in fighting personal addictions should be the greatest Power. When we are spiritually-minded, we seek ways to evade circumstances and places where we may revert to a carnal mind. At times, this may even require counseling to help us implement God's will.

When we are spiritually-minded, we avoid dead end futures in exchange for a peaceful eternity. This eternal peace always taller than physical or emotional satisfaction that is always temporary. Let us seek to recognize the addictions that weaken us. Let us become spiritually-minded and find peace. Let us pray to embrace the fruit of self-control in all facets of our lives.

Day 97

_____

_____

_____

_____

_____

_____

_____

_____

_____

_____

_____

_____

_____

_____

_____

<u>Self-Control</u>   Day 98

Watch and pray, lest you enter into temptation. The spirit indeed is willing, but the flesh is weak.

Mark 14:38   Matthew 26:41

How many times have we promised to begin doing something we believe to be good? Whether to eat better, exercise more, or even to get more rest, we often recognize positive changes that we can make in our lives. Conversely, there are also times that we commit ourselves to never doing something again? Indeed, many Christians have temporarily broken from the addictions of their eyes, hearts, bodies, or mouths, but find themselves once more overcome by temptation. Though willing and full of good intentions, we often encounter our weaknesses in the midst of our efforts to progress forward.

Jesus prescribed a simple formula for victory over our weaknesses - "watch and pray." For some, "watch" may mean to "watch out" for the triggers that come in various forms such as certain old friends, books, magazines, websites, restaurants, or emotional vulnerabilities. Let us not forget that when we pray and remain focused, we can maintain self-control. We can keep our minds on the One who will give us strength and guide us away from the pull of our weakened flesh.

Just like the disciples who grew weary when they were physically present with Jesus, we too may struggle with the things that tempt us. We will have victories and defeats. However, let us continue to watch and pray for Christ's guidance, so that we may have self-control and strength through Christ.

Day 98

_____

_____

_____

_____

_____

_____

_____

_____

_____

_____

_____

_____

_____

_____

_____

_____

Self-Control   Day 99

> *The lamp of the body is the eye. If therefore your eye is good, your whole body will be full of light.*

Matthew 6:22

Many children sing songs (both spiritual and secular) without recognizing the adult content contained in the lyrics. One such song is "Be Careful Little Eyes" (What You See). This song describes how small exposure to inappropriate things may later develop into larger problems. The musical group Casting Crowns described this as a "Slow Fade." [16]

How many of us have experienced the slow fade from a momentary temptation that eventually led to sin? How many have gazed with envy that led to hate, told small lies that led to betrayal, or maintained a secret friendship that led to an emotional affair. We can slowly fade in a variety of ways.

When we draw close to temptation, we may find it difficult to readjust our eyes or minds away from that which is ungodly. We soon find our minds, money, and bodies out of place. Yes, we strive to close our eyes and ears to these trappings; yet, the best way to control our exposure is to control our proximity to the things that lead us close to sin.

Like a farmer plowing a field, let us keep our eyes on a fixed target so that we will follow a straight path. With Christ as our target, we can avoid distractions. As children sing, "be careful little eyes what you see," let us set our

---

[16] Casting Crowns, *Slow Fade* (The Altar and the Door, 2007).

sights on Christ and the life God intended for us.

Day 99

_____

_____

_____

_____

_____

_____

_____

_____

_____

_____

_____

_____

_____

_____

_____

_____

_____

<u>Self-Control</u>   Day 100

> [12] *For we do not wrestle against flesh and blood, but against principalities, against powers, against the rulers of the darkness of this age, against spiritual hosts of wickedness in the heavenly places. [13] Therefore take up the whole armor of God, that you may be able to withstand in the evil day, and having done all, to stand.*

Ephesians 6:12-13

Many kids and teenagers struggle with discovering and establishing their own identity. While developing their identities, they encounter pressures from peers and friends. These friends typically splinter off in various directions as they grow older. Meanwhile, parents hope and pray that as their children become more independent, they will choose to go along with their positive peers. Parents also desire that their children remember the lessons taught at home once they are on their own and being tested.

As believers, we have opportunities to reveal that we have embraced the teachings of our heavenly Father. We face choices of whether to stand firm on His Word or to conveniently adopt common beliefs which we know do not align with His Word. Each of us can establish our identity as a follower of Christ or as someone who supports principles contrary to Christ. Whether by taking a stand on an issue or by simply conducting ourselves like Christ, we can reveal to the world on whose side we stand.

As we recognize our free will, acknowledge our legal opportunities, or even defend our legal rights, let us not allow our lives to endorse behaviors that contradict Christ. Let us withstand temptations to follow popular opinions, only to forsake the ways of Christ. While we love others in word and deed, let us learn to withstand principles that are contrary to our God.

Day 100

Reveal Your Fruit

> *[11] But thou, O man of God, flee these things; and follow after righteousness, godliness, faith, love, patience, meekness.   [12] Fight the good fight of faith, lay hold on eternal life, whereunto thou art also called, and hast professed a good profession before many witnesses. [13] I give thee charge in the sight of God, who quickeneth all things, and before Christ Jesus, who before Pontius Pilate witnessed a good confession; [14] That thou keep this commandment without spot, unrebukable, until the appearing of our Lord Jesus Christ.*

1 Timothy 6:11-14

In Psalm 119:105, David declares that the Lord's Word is a "lamp unto my feet and a light unto my path." Many of us also make the same verbal declaration. It is our life story, however, that will reveal whether our heart's ultimate guiding light is God or our own personal desires.

We are not perfect like Christ. We all have fallen, at

times. We were born into this sinful world prepared to sin and ready to follow our own desires. We all have sinned and experienced moments of choosing our desires over God's ways.

Nevertheless, what do our lives and aspirations indicate about us in the present? Are we walking through a dead end, crooked abyss, trying to fulfill and satisfy our every want? Are we ready and prepared to move to the next page of life and follow a path guided by the Spirit?

As we endeavor to live a life that is pleasing to God, Paul reminds us in 1 Timothy Chapter 6 that we should not do so passively. Instead of casually turning away from sin, Paul encourages us to do so *actively,* as if fleeing or escaping. Instead of just exercising our faith, we are directed to do so as if we are *fighting*. In other words, if we are committed to *grasping* eternal life, we should not be ashamed, embarrassed, or too cool about Christ as our focus.

Therefore, let us *wholeheartedly* commit ourselves to the One who died that we may have the right to eternal life. Let us *commit* to Christ and receive the Holy Spirit. When we receive the Spirit, our life stories will show that no matter our failures, we endeavored to "*Reveal the Fruit of the Spirit*" in our lives.

Day 101

_____

_____

_____

_____

_____

_____

_____

_____

_____

_____

_____

_____

_____

_____

_____

_____

_____

_____

_____

_____